MARCH

My Devotions®

Daily Readings for Young Christians

Contributors to the March devotions:

Lisa Clark, ~~~~~~~~~~~~~ Christine Ross,
Doris

VOL. 55 **MARCH–MAY 2013** **NO. 3**

F
R
I
D
A
Y

Power to Stay on Top

"I need two strong volunteers," Mr. Hernandez told his Sunday School class. Eager hands went up as the teacher pushed a small sturdy box into the room.

"Nick, will you stand on top of this box? And Jason, please stand next to the box." The other students giggled. The boys took their places.

"Good," said Mr. Hernandez. "Now, Nick, you pull Jason up. Jason, you pull Nick down."

Looking a little nervous, the boys joined hands. After a few moments of pushing and pulling, Nick gave up and landed on his feet on the floor next to Jason.

"Thank you, gentlemen. What happened here?" the teacher asked.

"It really wasn't fair. Jason had gravity helping him pull Nick down," said Amy. "Nick never had much of a chance of winning."

Mr. Hernandez nodded. Then he said, "Sometimes, Christians find themselves in situations like Nick's. They believe they can hang out with friends who are headed for trouble and yet resist temptations to sin themselves. They might even believe they can change things for the better. But when you're with someone who is involved in sinful things, it's like being the one on top of the box. It's easier to be pulled down into sin than to pull up someone."

Today's verse from God's Word tells us to "be wise as serpents and innocent as doves." We can't always avoid people who are trapped in sinful living. God wants us to share the Good News about Jesus with those who don't know Him. We also need to be wise, asking God for His power to resist temptation. His Word makes us strong. His Word makes us wise.

Journal:

How can you be innocent as a dove around others who may not know Jesus? Why is it important to also be as wise as a snake in those situations?

Pray:

Heavenly Father, plant Your Word in me, that I may find my wisdom and strength in You. In Jesus' name I pray. Amen. D. N.

Isaiah 43:18–21

Water in the Desert

Try reading today's Bible verses aloud. Like poetry, they contain picture language.

Maybe as you read the verses you thought about the amazing story of Moses leading the people of Israel out of slavery. Soon after they left Egypt, Pharaoh changed his mind about letting them go. He sent his soldiers to chase the Israelites to the shore of the Red Sea. God was at work. He saved His people in a miraculous way. God parted the water, creating a path for the people to cross over to the other side. When they were across safely, the soldiers tried to follow. Then God released the water. The soldiers and their horses all drowned.

Today's reading tells us that just as God made a dry path in a sea, He can also make water in a desert. That's one of my favorite examples of picture language—water in a desert. Think of it!

What a powerful and loving God! The God who can make water in the desert is the same God who created each person to be different and special. He is the God who faithfully loves us even though we sin and are unfaithful to Him. He is the God who promised never to leave us. He is the God who hears every prayer and knows what we need before we ask. He is the God who has prepared a place for us in heaven. He is the God who sent His Son to redeem us from sin.

Christ's victory for us over sin, death, and the devil ensures us that God brings good out of bad situations. Our God solves impossible problems. He is with us every moment of our lives. He blesses our service to His glory. He is worthy of praise.

Journal:

Draw some desert plants enjoying a rainy day.

Pray:

Lord God, through Your Word, remind me how much You care for me. Thank You for forgiving me when I am unfaithful. In Jesus' name I pray. Amen.   D. N.

**S
U
N
D
A
Y**

Made New in Christ

When Jeremy was a young man, he didn't obey his parents or teachers. He hung around with friends who were a bad influence on him. He was often in trouble. One night, Jeremy and his friends stole a car. As he drove faster and faster, his friends laughed and celebrated. Suddenly, there was a loud crash, and everything went black.

When Jeremy woke up in the hospital, he learned that he had hit another car. The woman driving that car would be in a wheelchair for the rest of her life. A jury sent Jeremy to jail.

In jail, Jeremy had a lot of time to think about his life. A pastor who visited the jail became his friend. Pastor Colton told him about Jesus, who came to take away our sins. Jeremy studied God's Word and learned that Jesus died and rose again for him. He prayed, and he knew God forgave him because of Jesus.

On the day Jeremy got out of jail, Pastor Colton took him out for lunch. As they walked into the restaurant, Jeremy noticed a man in a wheelchair. This was a painful reminder that someone was in a wheelchair because of what he had done. He ran out the door in tears.

Pastor Colton followed and gently put his arms around Jeremy. "Even though God forgives you, there are still consequences for sin," said Pastor Colton. "Seeing someone in a wheelchair may always remind you of your sin. But it can also remind you of the great things God has done for you. Each time you see a wheelchair, thank God for the victory He gave you over your sin."

Journal:

What things remind you of your sins? How can these same things make you think of God's goodness? How does the cross remind us of both terrible and wonderful things?

Pray:

Father, let the forgiveness of my sins remind me of what Jesus has done for me. Thank You for the gift of new life in Baptism. Amen.   D. N.

MONDAY

God's Will

On Sunday afternoon, Grandma went into the hospital with a bad infection. When the family got home from visiting her, Mom said, "Let's pray that God will heal Grandma."

Haley bowed her head as the family prayed together. Then she looked up and said, "If God knows everything, then He knows if Grandma will get better, doesn't He?"

"Yes," Mom said quietly.

"Then why should we pray? Will praying change anything?"

"Oh, yes!" Mom said. "Prayer changes the prayer. Through prayer we see God's answer as well as His plan. There are places in the Bible where people prayed."

"I remember," said Haley. "We talked about King Hezekiah in Sunday School last week."

"That's right!" said Mom. "King Hezekiah had become very ill. The prophet Isaiah came to Hezekiah and told him that the Lord said Hezekiah would die and not recover from his illness. Hezekiah prayed to God for healing. Through the prophet Isaiah, the Lord told Hezekiah He had heard his prayers and that Hezekiah would recover and live another fifteen years.

"God does what is best in our lives. Grandma trusts Jesus for forgiveness. He has healed her of sin. We pray that she will be healed of this infection also. God hears our prayers and will answer them as He sees best."

Journal:

Begin a prayer list in this journal or elsewhere. Each day, list the things you pray about. Write down how God answers your prayers.

Pray:

Loving God, strengthen my faith through Your Word so that in faith, I pray for others and trust You in all things. In Jesus' name I pray. Amen.

D. N.

**T
U
E
S
D
A
Y**

The Real Thing

John was taking care of his younger cousin Alex for the afternoon. They walked to the corner store for a treat. When they went to the register to pay, little Alex surprised John. He pulled a play five-dollar bill from his pocket and said, "Let me pay for that."

The clerk smiled at the little boy. "Thanks, Alex," said John. "Maybe you should save your money. I'll pay for the juice."

"Okay," said Alex.

Why couldn't Alex use his money to pay for their juice? Because it wasn't the real thing. John had seen and used real money, so he easily recognized the real thing. He knew immediately that Alex's money was fake money.

Reading and learning about the real things in God's Word helps us to recognize false ideas. From the Bible, we learn that God is perfect and expects us to be perfect. We also learn that we are born in sin and can never be perfect. In His great love and mercy, God sent His own Son to take the punishment for our sin. Through His Word and in Baptism, God graciously gives us the forgiveness Jesus earned.

God's Word tells us the real story about life and salvation. It shows us that our sinful nature puts us first, leads us to get even, or wants us to do what seems right. With the Spirit's power, we come to know the real things of God and share the real Good News with others.

Journal:

What are the dangers of not knowing the truth about Jesus? Tell how the following will help you understand the real things of God: attending church and Sunday School, reading God's Word, praying, Christian friends.

Pray:

Through Your Spirit's power, lead me to know Your truth, dear God. Protect me from sin and the danger of fake ideas. I pray in Jesus' name. Amen. D. N.

Esther 4:13–14

For Such a Time as This

Do you know the Old Testament story of Queen Esther? Esther was a woman who lived in a foreign country called Babylon, where her people, the Jews, were slaves. When the king of Babylon married beautiful Esther, she became the queen.

An evil man named Haman tricked the king into passing a law that would mean death for many Jews. It seemed that Esther was the only one who could persuade the king to save the Jews. Yet Esther was afraid that by speaking out she might anger the king and also be sentenced to die.

Then Esther's uncle Mordecai encouraged her with these words: "And who knows whether you have not come to the kingdom for such a time as this?" (v. 14). Mordecai was suggesting that perhaps God had made Esther queen so she could save her people.

The story has a happy ending. God gave Esther courage to go before the king. He had mercy on God's people. In the end, it was evil Haman who was put to death.

Like the Jews in Esther's time, we also have been given a death sentence. Because of our sin, we are guilty before God, our King, of breaking His laws. We deserve eternal punishment.

Rejoice! God has provided our story a happy ending! In His great love, God sent His Son into the world "for such a time as this." Jesus lived a perfect life in our place and died on the cross to pay for our sins. Because of Jesus, we have been granted forgiveness and are now His royal sons and daughters!

Journal:

Consider how you are like Esther. Why do you think God placed you in your family? in your school? with certain friends? In what special way might you serve in His kingdom?

Pray:

Dear Father in heaven, forgive me when I don't think the work I do is important. Use me, O Lord, to help others in Your name. I pray in Jesus' name. Amen.   D. N.

7 Revelation 3:2–3

THURSDAY

Strengthen What Remains

The weather forecaster had predicted severe storms. The clouds twisted into a tornado funnel and moved along the ground. Within moments, the buildings and trees in its path were reduced to piles of rubble. Then the storm was gone. Over.

Shocked families returned from school and work to the neighborhood mess. Finding even little things that hadn't been destroyed—a photograph, a special dish, a piece of jewelry—was reason for joy. These little things helped the survivors go on. People would build new homes and lives, strengthened by their connections to the past. Life would go on.

Life can be full of trouble. Troubles can be small, like homework that is too hard or toys that break. Troubles can be overwhelming, like the death of someone we love, a terrible accident, family troubles, or the loss of everything we own in a fire or storm.

Trouble is in the world because of sin. Jesus, the Son of God, came into the world to deal with trouble. When He died on the cross, He made a way for us out of trouble and into a right relationship with God. Someday, we will live with Him forever.

While we are in the world, we will face troubles. Yet even in times of terrible trouble, Jesus gives us the strength to begin again. In His Word, God tells us, "I am the Alpha and the Omega, the beginning and the end" (Revelation 21:6). He is the connection that will take us from a troubled past to a brighter future.

When you have troubles, you can trust God to strengthen you with His never-failing love and forgiveness. "Remember, then, what you received and heard" (Revelation 3:3). And by God's grace, go on!

Journal:

Memorize this psalm verse: "God is our refuge and strength, a very present help in trouble" (Psalm 46:1).

Pray:

Dear God, You are my strength and help. Lead me to look to You when troubles come. In Jesus' name I pray. Amen.   D. N.

Matthew 23:11–12

Who's the Greatest?

Let's talk about the biggest and best.
Fill in the lines below.

The greatest hockey player is _____.

The greatest musician is_____.

The greatest scientist is _____.

The greatest teacher is _____.

The greatest dishwasher is _____.

The greatest garbage taker-outer is _____.

Do you worry about being the best athlete, the smartest student, or an admired musician? It's easy to think others love us because we write creative stories, have the best looks, or sing in an elite choir.

Those who lived during Jesus' time wanted to be the biggest and best too. Sure, God would love people who were powerful, rich, popular, or very religious. But Jesus reminds us that this is not how He judges greatness.

It's just the opposite. In today's Bible reading, our Lord says, "The greatest among you shall be your servant. Whoever exalts himself will be humbled, and whoever humbles himself will be exalted."

Those who are humble are great? This is definitely not what most people or adults think! But the God who made the largest flower and the fanciest bird isn't concerned about appearances. He gives you a childlike faith and a desire in your heart to serve. He gives you this attitude by His Spirit, who works through the Gospel message: "For even the Son of Man came not to be served but to serve, and to give His life as a ransom for many" (Mark 10:45).

Journal:

Who has served you today? Make a list. Thank God for each one. If possible, thank those people too.

Pray:

Dear Jesus, forgive me when I find my identity in being better than others rather than in being Your child. Amen.   D. S.

2 Corinthians 2:14

Journey with Jesus

The Scout troop had several meetings to plan their first hike. They gathered supplies needed to make the hike safe and successful. The boys also invited some older Scouts, who were experienced hikers, to help them plan and to hike with them.

They contacted a forest ranger, who gave them a guidebook. That book laid out trails to follow. It showed places to rest and get water. It also marked places to avoid. The ranger gave them his cell-phone number. He told them how to reach him if they needed help while hiking.

When they packed their gear and backpacks, the Scouts made sure they had everything they needed. They were careful not to take extra things that would add weight and tire them out. A big celebration was planned at the place where the hike would end.

We are in the Church Year season of Lent. During the forty days of Lent, we follow Jesus on His journey to the cross. We remember Jesus' suffering and death for us. Lent ends on Easter Sunday, when we celebrate Jesus' resurrection from the dead. Lent is also a time for believers to think about sins and to confess those sins, which weigh us down and make our journey through life difficult.

God, our heavenly Father, is our guide on this life journey. He gives us His Word, the Bible, to strengthen us. He is with us in our Baptism, protecting us from sin, death, and the devil. Along the way, we are in constant communication with Him through prayer. Our lives are blessed by other believers who encourage and help us as we travel.

Our earthly journey of faith will end when we die. Then begins an everlasting celebration in heaven with Jesus, our Savior!

Journal:

What has been the best part of your faith journey? When have you lost your way or met a roadblock?

Pray:

Dear Jesus, You are my Savior from sin and death. May Your Spirit guide me through life's journey. I pray in Your name. Amen.   D. N.

Doubts Answered

Even before his birth, John the Baptist's whole life was linked to Jesus. John was born only a few months before Jesus. The two men were related. John was chosen and sent by God to prepare the people of Jesus' day for the coming of the Christ. From the banks of the Jordan River, John proclaimed that people should repent and be baptized. One day, Jesus also came to be baptized. John told the crowd that Jesus was the Savior for whom they had been looking.

John was such a fearless and determined preacher that he spoke against the sin of King Herod, and Herod had John thrown into prison.

While John sat in prison, he may have wondered if Jesus really was who He said He was. John had baptized and touched Jesus, yet now he needed encouragement.

John turned to Jesus for answers. John sent some of his followers to ask Jesus if He really was the Messiah they had expected.

Jesus gave John proof. Tell John that "the blind receive their sight and the lame walk, lepers are cleansed and the deaf hear, and the dead are raised up, and the poor have good news preached to them" (v. 5). We can hope that John's faith that Jesus was the Savior grew stronger.

The feeling of doubt can be a kind of prison. What causes you to doubt God's love and care? Does loneliness make you forget that the Savior who died for you will provide everything you need? Do troubles make you wonder if God is really there? Is it hard to trust that God forgives your sins? Has someone tried to convince you that your faith in Jesus is foolish?

Like John, we can go to Jesus for the answers. In His Word are many promises and the sure hope of eternal life.

Journal:
In your journal, write "Jesus is the answer to my doubt."

Pray:
Dear Jesus, thank You for Your constant loving care, even when I doubt You. Forgive me and strengthen me with Your Holy Spirit. I am trusting You for everything. Amen.   D. N.

The Treasure Is Yours

It's 8:00 a.m. Seimone ties her shoes, gulps down her orange juice, and stuffs her books into her backpack. A bit later, a loud wail comes from her bedroom. "Where is it? Dad! Mom! I can't find my book report, and it's due today!" And so the frantic search begins.

8:02—Look under bed. Find candy wrapper, but no book report.

8:05—Check kitchen table, where report was last night. See only orange juice pitcher and cereal bowl.

8:10—Time to leave for school. Seimone sadly opens the refrigerator to get her lunch and screams, joyfully this time, "I found it! I stuck it into the refrigerator instead of the juice."

Have you ever lost homework, a baseball glove, or a shoe? I'm sure you were just as excited as Seimone when you found what you had lost. That experience is like discovering a hidden treasure.

Jesus told a story about a man who did just that. Finding a hidden treasure in a field, the man sold everything, took the money, and bought the field and the treasure.

What treasure was so important that someone would give up everything for it? The apostle Paul knew. Paul gave up many things—his home, position, friends—when he came to know Christ. Once Paul was connected to Jesus, he said everything in his past was like garbage. Being joined to Christ by faith in His death and resurrection and having the gift of eternal life was now Paul's treasure.

You have received the same treasure through the power of God's Spirit. You can truthfully say, "Jesus is my Lord and my Savior."

Journal:

Write how you feel when you know that Jesus has searched for you and found you and made you His own.

Pray:

Lord Jesus, You are my greatest treasure. I rejoice that You have found me and made me Yours in Baptism. Amen.   D. S.

13

T
U
E
S
D
A
Y

Victory Guaranteed

"Lucy!" Ava yelled as the end-of-school bell rang. "What did you get on your English test? I got an A . . . again! It was *sooooo* easy."

"Want to come over and play my new game?" Ava continued. "Bet you can't get to the fourth level yet."

"I've got a good idea, Lucy. Let's race to my house. I know I can beat you."

Lucy sighed. "Ava, all you care about is winning. Can't we just have fun?"

How do you feel about competition? Some people think competition is bad. Instead of concentrating only on winning and beating others, they think it is more important to have fun and improve skills.

Others ask, "What's wrong with keeping score?" They say competition is a part of life and helps you achieve more, to be the best you can be.

There are ways to combine cooperation and competition. As part of a team, you have the opportunity to help your teammates and win together. Cheering for both the winners and the losers encourages everyone to do their best.

How is it in our Christian life? Do we compete with one another or cooperate? Thanks to our Savior's victory, we don't have to worry about winning. He's won salvation for us! Because Jesus defeated death, hell, and Satan for us on the cross, we're guaranteed the crown of life. "Thanks be to God, who gives us the victory through our Lord Jesus Christ" (1 Corinthians 15:57).

Knowing this, we encourage others to take hold of the prize offered to all. We want everyone to be victorious because God Himself wants everyone to be saved.

Journal:

How do you feel when you're a winner? a loser? How is your attitude toward life affected by the victory God gives you?

Pray:

Father, thank You for Your Spirit, who gives me power to live. Thank You for sending Jesus to win eternal life for me. Amen.   D. S.

Psalm 37:23–24

Safe in God's Hands

The sixth graders were doing a science experiment. Each team designed a box that would keep a raw egg from breaking when it was dropped from the second floor balcony onto the school parking lot.

Jeremy and his team wrapped the egg in Bubble Wrap, put it in the box, and then wrapped more bubble wrap around the outside. Jaden's team filled the box with a container of gelatin, which gelled around the egg. Macy's team surrounded the egg with packing peanuts.

One by one the eggs were dropped, and the boxes were opened. The eggs fell a long way, but not a single one was broken! The boxes protected them.

The Bible tells God's people they are safe in the hands of God. When we are in God's hands, it doesn't matter if we are sleeping in bed, riding in a car, flying in an airplane, playing with friends, taking a test, or even fighting in a war. God protects us in the best way—in His hands. Dangers may come. Sorrow may come. But through it all, God is our support.

Jesus' strong hands were nailed to the cross so He could die and take away our sins. With His sacrifice, He defeated the powers of death and the devil. On the cross and at the empty tomb, we see His eternal care for us. Through His Word, we hear His promise also to care for us while we are here on earth, in our classroom, with our family and friends.

When you feel afraid, remember the words of today's Bible reading. You are safe in God's strong and loving hands.

Journal:

Name a place or a time you feel frightened. How can you remind yourself that even there or then you are in God's hands?

Pray:

Dear heavenly Father, thank You for taking care of me wherever I go. When I am afraid or fall, remind me of Your promise to keep me in Your loving hands. In Jesus' name I pray. Amen.   C. S.

THURSDAY

Days of Thunder

Many years ago, the people of northern Europe named a day of the week after their god Thor. They believed that Thor sent rain for the crops and created thunder by beating his hammer against an anvil. Eventually, Thor's Day became known as Thursday.

It's easy to imagine thunder sounding like a hammer. Does thunder ever sound like God's voice to you? One day, a crowd listened to Jesus explain that soon He would die. Jesus wanted to give glory to God by doing what the Father wanted, so He said, "Father, glorify Your name" (v. 28).

God spoke from heaven, "I have glorified it, and I will glorify it again" (v. 28).

Do you know what the crowd heard? Many of them thought the voice from heaven was only thunder. The people weren't willing to listen to God and understand His will.

Jesus heard God's voice. He knew God wanted Him to die and rise again for us. And it's very Good News for us that Jesus did this— He gained our salvation!

Do you ever hear God speaking? Perhaps you wonder whether to go outside and play ball or stay inside and help your brother or sister with homework. Suddenly, it starts to rain, and that could be God's answer. God can also speak through Christian friends, parents, pastors, and teachers when we need advice.

But there's no more certain way to hear God's voice than to read the Bible. There, in His Word, we find God's message of eternal life through faith in His Son, Jesus.

Journal:

Think of an important decision you might need to make. What word from God might help you?

Pray:

Dear Jesus, give me ears to hear Your voice in Your Word and, through Your Spirit, work in my life to do Your will. Amen.   D. S.

Romans 7:18–19

Who's in Charge?

Four-year-old Victor sat in the principal's office. Victor had bitten another child. "Tell me what happened," said Mr. Robbins.

"My brain tells me what to do," said Victor.

"Yes," said Mr. Robbins, "and your brain needs to tell your teeth not to bite people."

"This tooth and this tooth listen," explained Victor, pointing to the front of his mouth, "but the rest don't pay any attention!"

Victor was making excuses. Although his excuses weren't the truth, he said something interesting. Not one of us listens to God's Word and does everything right. Even when we try, we sin. We were born in sin. The Bible calls that condition our "sinful nature."

When our brain tells our hands not to hit, our feet not to kick, or our mouth not to gossip, we might fail. When we think about trying to be good boys and girls by doing everything right, we can't. Does our condition change God's demand for our perfection? No, not one little bit. That's why it is such a relief to find out that Jesus did everything right for us. He listened and obeyed His Father's words and will. Every thought and every feeling of His was perfect for us. Even when He spread His arms on the cross and felt the nails drive into His flesh, He did not sin.

Jesus offers His goodness and perfection to His children. Through His Word and in Baptism, He gives us faith to believe that He is our Savior. Through His Spirit, He offers us the forgiveness of sins and daily opportunities to use our brain, feet, hands, arms, and teeth in service to others. Each day, guided by God's love, we can join Victor in serving others in love. We can say we're sorry when we sin.

Journal:

What sin or bad habit do you want to stop doing? Write a prayer asking God to forgive you and give you power to change your life.

Pray:

Dear God, thank You for loving me even when I sin. Guide me and give me power to do the good things You have for me to do. Amen.   C. S.

16 Jeremiah 1:4–5

Love at First Sight

Michaela was two weeks old when her grandma saw her for the first time. Grandma picked up the baby and held her in. She rocked her and made funny baby noises. She sang to her and prayed for her. She looked deep into her eyes.

Michaela was too tiny to do much, but she looked back into her grandma's eyes. Michaela curved her little lips into what looked like a smile. She snuggled into her grandma's arms and gurgled.

Grandma was in love.

How could she love this little girl so much, this person whom she had known for such a short time? The baby didn't do anything to earn her grandma's love. She couldn't walk or talk or give her grandma presents. But her grandma loved her just because—just because she existed—just because she was a part of her family. Just because.

That's the way God loves us. He loved us before we were born, before anyone knew what we looked like. He loved us whether or not we would be good at sports or get straight As in school. He loved us when we looked cute and cuddly. He loves us when we aren't so cute, when we make mistakes, when we sin. He will also love us when we are old.

How can God love us so much when He knows so much bad stuff about us? He loves us because He made us. He loves us because Jesus made it possible for us to be part of His family. He loves us not because of anything we do, but because God is love.

God so loved us that He sent Jesus to be our Savior. God made a way for us to live with Him forever. That's how valuable we are to Him. God is in love with us. Always.

Journal:

Who models God's love for you? Thank that person. Then thank God for that person. To whom can you model God's love?

Pray:

Dear Father in heaven, thank You for loving me all the time. Help me remember that I am Your precious child. Amen.   C. S.

Acts 16:9–10

Listening for God's Voice

Do you remember the name of anyone in the Bible who heard a message from God in the night? One night, St. Paul saw a vision. In it, a man from Macedonia (now Greece) called, "Come over to Macedonia and help us" (v. 9). Paul knew God wanted him to go. Many became Christians because of his work there.

Today, many people celebrate St. Patrick's Day. Although most people know little about his life, Patrick was another man who heard God speak.

When Patrick was a teenager, he was captured by Irish raiders and taken from his family in England to be a slave in Ireland. For six years, he took care of his master's sheep and pigs, until he finally escaped Ireland by boat.

Patrick was glad to be home again. Then one night, he dreamed of an angel and Irish people calling, "We ask you, come and walk among us once more." Patrick didn't want to go back to Ireland, but he believed God was calling him. As a result, schools and churches were built, and many Irish people turned from the gods of the sun, wind, and sea and followed the one true God.

God's voice is heard through His Word. That voice encourages us to share our faith with others no matter how difficult that may seem. It We may be afraid and not know what to say. Paul, Patrick, and every other Christian at times has felt the same way. Yet You can let others know about Jesus, who paid for the sins of everybody in the world. Wherever God has placed you, He put you there for a reason—it's your Ireland.

Journal:

Ask a parent, teacher, pastor, or other Christian adult how God is working in his or her life. Write about your conversation in your journal.

Pray:

Dear Lord, Your voice leads, strengthens, and encourages. Be with missionaries everywhere and with me in my mission spot. Amen.   D. S.

MONDAY

Strong and Courageous

Riley often felt afraid. If her mom was late to pick her up from school, her stomach tightened. Given enough time, the tight feeling crept up into her throat, and she felt like crying. Riley hated feeling this way, but she didn't know how to stop.

One night, Riley's parents were late getting home. Even while Riley played a card game with her babysitter, she felt a "pit" in her stomach. She listened carefully for her parents' car in the driveway. Her sitter must have sensed Riley's anxiety.

"Have I told you how I first knew without a doubt that God was real?" Sarah asked.

Surprised, Riley raised her eyes from her cards, "I don't think so," she responded.

Sarah shared, "I used to feel afraid."

"You did?" Riley was surprised.

"Uh huh. A friend told me to memorize Joshua 1:9. A few months later, my fiancé broke up with me. I waited to feel afraid and anxious, but I felt calm. I remembered the words of that verse, 'Be strong and courageous. Do not be frightened, and do not be dismayed, for the LORD your God is with you wherever you go.' Jesus, my Lord and Savior, was with me right then! I already believed, but at that moment I really knew He was at work, comforting me. I knew that His Word was powerful and that faith in Jesus made a lifelong difference!"

Riley's eyes welled up with tears of comfort and joy. She was thankful Sarah had shared this special experience. Riley believed God's promise was for her too. Just as Riley realized she wasn't afraid anymore, she heard a car door. Guess who was home?

Journal:

Draw a picture of a fearful situation. Draw Jesus beside you.

Pray:

Dear Jesus, thank You for being with me in all situations. When troubles come, give me a calm heart and trusting faith. Amen.   C. R.

Voices of Love

When Mom speaks my first and middle names together, she is demanding my obedience. If I am running to catch a ball before it rolls into the street and Dad shouts my nickname, he means, "Be careful!"

What do your parents sound like when they want you to obey? to be careful? to tell you they love you?

Do you know that God knows your name? He wants you to listen to His voice.

In the past, God spoke to His people through prophets, priests, and kings such as Moses, Samuel, and King David. God's people listened to these leaders to learn God's Law and to be reminded of God's rules. Just like a parent, God wants His children to obey Him.

Today, God speaks to you through the Bible. Scripture is called the Word of God. God also calls you through His only Son. Jesus' life and death shouts out that your heavenly Father loves you. God cares so much that He sent Jesus to die so your disobedience is forgiven.

When you were baptized, you became God's child. Since then, God's Holy Spirit has been working to guard your faith and help you hear God's voice. Jesus promises that when you believe in Him as God's Son and your Savior, you know His voice. You will grow in your ability to understand Scripture. You are able talk directly to God in prayer.

What an incredible heavenly Father you have! One who loves you, calls you by name, and speaks to you.

Journal:

Write about what God said to you through this Bible reading and devotion.

Pray:

Heavenly Father, thank You for sending Jesus to be my Good Shepherd. Through Your Holy Spirit, help me listen to His voice and follow Him. Amen.
                                                                    C. R.

WEDNESDAY

Rock Solid

For the fifth day in a row, Sam's family sat around his aunt's dinner table. Last week, Sam's home was destroyed in a flood. Sam, his parents, and his younger brother had moved in with his aunt.

After dinner, Aunt Sally handed a devotion book to Sam's dad. As he skimmed the devotion, his eyes filled with tears. Then he said, "This devotion was written just for us!" Dad read Matthew 7:24–29 aloud and then started singing this familiar hymn stanza:

> *His oath, His covenant and blood*
> *Support me in the raging flood;*
> *When ev'ry earthly prop gives way,*
> *He then is all my hope and stay.*
> *On Christ, the solid rock, I stand;*
> *All other ground is sinking sand.* (LSB *575/576:3*)

The family joined in. Then Mom said, "I've hummed that hymn all week." Then she took a small rock from her pocket and set it on the table for all to see. "One day last week, I walked away from our ruined furniture on the trash heap," said Mom. "As I looked out over the field of mud, I sang this same hymn. It comforted me to know Christ sustains us through difficult times now and forever. This rock was on the ground where I was singing and praying. Since then, I've carried it in my pocket. Every time I feel it there or see it, I thank Jesus for being our Rock. Then I ask Him to send this family to other hurting people so we can share the story of His love with them."

In all life's troubles, we can lean on Jesus, our Rock and our Redeemer. He has overcome all our enemies. Through faith, He gives us the hope of heaven, a brand new home.

Journal:
Draw a large rock in your journal and write the name "Christ" on it.

Pray:
Father, thank You for Jesus. When problems flood my life, sustain me through Him. Give me comfort and hope. In His name I pray. Amen. C. R.

Millstones

Mrs. Murray asked the fourth grade Sunday School students to share a favorite Bible story. Jenny's hand shot up!

Mrs. Murray smiled at Jenny's enthusiasm and said, "Go ahead, Jenny."

"My favorite story is when Jesus told the disciples to welcome children. If anyone taught children to sin, Jesus said it would be better that they have a millstone tied around their neck and be drowned in the sea," Jenny declared.

Mrs. Murray commented, "That's an unusual favorite. What made you choose it?"

"Last summer, my parents and I toured in Israel. We saw lots of millstones. They are donut-shaped rocks. Some were taller and wider than me! Even the small ones were too heavy for me to pick up. They had to be heavy to crush grain into flour," Jenny explained.

"While we stood next to an old mill, the tour guide read the Scripture verses about how it would be better to be drowned by a millstone than to cause a child to sin. She said she knows of parents who teach their children to lie in order to get money from wealthy people. She said that in some countries there are people who steal children and treat them like slaves! Then she pointed to the millstones and said, 'But God loves children so very much that He has warned adults of the terrible consequences of teaching children evil ways.'

"I remember looking at the stones and thinking how intense God's love is for me. This loving God sent His Son to die for the sins of all people, not just adults. He tells them to welcome children and to learn from our trusting faith. Now when I think of a millstone, I know I am loved by God and am important to Jesus!"

Journal:
Describe a time when you realized how much God loved you.

Pray:
Dear Jesus, help all the children of the world learn about Your saving love. Use me to be a friend to those near me. Amen.   C. R.

FRIDAY

Perfect Love

To better understand 1 Corinthians 13:4–6, replace all the nouns and pronouns in the verses with your name. For example, if your name is Cory, you will read "Cory is patient and kind . . ."

Slowly read out loud the following and say your name wherever there is a line, and see if it is true.

"___ is patient and kind; ___ does not envy or boast; ___ is not arrogant or rude. ___ does not insist on [his or her] own way; ___ is not irritable or resentful; ___ does not rejoice at wrongdoing, but ___ rejoices with the truth. ___ bears all things, believes all things, hopes all things, endures all things."

Are any of the statements you read 100 percent true?

Now go back to what you just read aloud and reread it. This time, read the name *Jesus* in all the blanks. For example: "Jesus is patient and kind."

Now everything you said is true! Jesus *is* patient with people. Jesus did not insist on His own way. Jesus did only what His Father wanted Him to do. Jesus greatly rejoices in truth. Jesus endured difficulties, even death on a cross.

Through Jesus, we see what true love looks like. Because of Jesus' perfect love, He carried our unloving thoughts and action to the cross.

By God's grace in Jesus, we are forgiven our many unloving actions. Because Jesus loves us perfectly, the Holy Spirit helps us show love to others.

Journal:

Write about how reading your name into the Scripture passage made you feel. Silly? Sad? Proud? How did reading Jesus' name make you feel?

Pray:

Jesus, Your life, death, and resurrection are proof of Your great love. Teach me to understand Your love. May Your Holy Spirit lead me to love others, especially those who do not know Your love. Amen.   C. R.

Ephesians 6:16–18

The ACTS of Prayer

The letters *ACTS* can help you understand what Scripture means when it says to pray "with all prayer and supplication" (v. 18).

Each letter of ACTS is connected with a kind of prayer. The *A* is for *Adoration*. You can begin a time of prayer by adoring or praising God. "God, I praise You for making this beautiful world. You are wonderful. You are almighty and perfect." Praising is telling God the good things about Him and the good things He has done.

Another kind of prayer is *Confession*. In confession, you repent of your sins. You tell God you are sorry for the things you have done wrong. If you have trouble thinking of specific sins, think about how your actions compare to God's actions. Are you almighty or perfect? Are you holy and patient like God is? The Bible tells us that when we repent of sin, "[God] is faithful and just to forgive us our sins" (1 John 1:9).

Now you can *Thank* God for the forgiveness you received through His Son, Jesus. What else are you thankful for? You might thank God for family members, friends, an opportunity to play on a sports team, the sunshine, or the rain. You can be thankful for anything God has done in the world or in your life.

The final type of prayer in ACTS is *Supplication*. Supplication is the most common prayer request. Here you ask God to *supply* for other peoples' needs and for your own needs. God wants you to bring every worry, care, or request to Him in prayer.

Journal:

Write a prayer using ACTS to help guide you.

Pray:

Father God, thank You for inviting me to pray and for hearing every single prayer of mine. Thank You, Jesus, for teaching me and all Your children how to pray. In Your name I pray. Amen.   C. R.

Today's Parade

Everyone loves to watch a parade or be in one! Pets, floats, marching bands, horses, cars—sometimes even the military file by.

Every New Year's Day, you can enjoy the Rose Parade. The beautiful floats are decorated with roses and other flowers. Hundreds of thousands of visitors line the streets of Pasadena, California, to watch. They wave hats or flags at their favorite float and sing along with the marching bands. They yell, clap, and have fun.

Imagine a parade of one person riding on a donkey. This happened the day Jesus went into the city of Jerusalem on the first Palm Sunday. Many people believed that Jesus was the promised Messiah who had come to save them. The people would not let Jesus walk quietly into the city. They wanted a parade, so they started one!

Instead of waving flags, the people pulled branches off the nearest palm trees and shouted, "Hosanna!" (*Hosanna* means "Save us now!") They also cried out, "Blessed is He who comes in the name of the Lord, even the King of Israel" (v. 13).

Jesus is not like any other king. He came as a humble servant to rule over our hearts by dying on a cross for our sins just five days after the parade. King Jesus also rose from the dead. Now He lives and rules over all things.

Back then, people shouted, waved, danced, and sang as Jesus came by. Maybe that's the kind of energy you saw or heard in today's church service. In the reading of His Word and giving of His Sacraments, King Jesus comes again and again to save us from all our enemies. He comes to rule in our hearts and lives. He comes to give us the hope of heaven.

Journal:

Draw a processional cross you would like to see used in your church.

Pray:

Lord Jesus, as King, You rule over all creation, You protect Your Church, including me, and You promise to rescue me from every evil. I am humbled by Your love. Thank You, Jesus. Amen.   C. R.

2 Timothy 4:8

MONDAY

A Lasting Crown

"Hosanna! Hosanna! Hosanna!" Taylor was waving two palm branches from yesterday's church service.

"Will you cut that out?!" Kole yelled. Kole was not in the mood for his little sister's parade. "Besides, look at those branches. They're falling apart all over the place and making a mess." Kole looked up and saw Mom staring at him. Her look was a mixture of disappointment and worry.

Heaving a sigh, Kole told her, "Look, Mom, I'm sorry. But I just can't get this project to look right, and Taylor's distracting me. I'll never win that geography trophy. Nothing's going the way I planned."

"I have a question for you," Mom said. Kole set down his glue and turned toward her. "How long do you think that geography trophy will last?"

Kole smiled a little. "Probably longer than the soccer one from last year—the pieces are still in my room somewhere. But definitely longer than Taylor's palm branches!"

Mom chuckled. "You know, it's great to do your best. It can also be fun to win. But the best prize of all has already been won for you."

Kole had heard this before. "Heaven, right?"

"Some Bible verses describe a crown of life or a treasure that never fades away," Mom added.

"Yeah, I remember that," said Kole. "And on Palm Sunday, people called Jesus the King of Israel. It's hard to believe that a few days later He wore a crown of thorns."

"It surely surprised the disciples, but that week went exactly as God planned, and Jesus won the crown of life for us all."

Journal:
Are you proud of a certain award? How does it feel to know God will give you the crown of life?

Pray:
Dear God, thank You for Jesus, the King of kings, and my lasting crown. Amen.
L. C.

26 1 Peter 5:6–7

T
U
E
S
D
A
Y

Jesus' Love

How are you feeling today? Are you excited for Easter fun? Are you worried about grades this time of year? Are you anxious about making the team for spring or summer sports? Maybe your feelings are so strong right now that you're not sure how to describe them.

During Jesus' last week before the cross, He experienced many things. On Palm Sunday, He must have been thrilled with the people's praise. Later, He was furious at people who cared more about money than about respecting God's temple.

In the Garden of Gethsemane, Jesus struggled with what He was about to go through—the pain of the cross and the sin of every person for all time. Then He was betrayed by someone close to Him. (Do you remember his name?) He was denied by one of His best friends. (How about his name?) He was bullied and mocked by people who were on His side just a few days earlier. How terrible this all must have felt! On the cross, He was completely alone.

You know what? No matter how *you* feel, there is one thing Jesus *always* feels for you: love. He loves you, and He knows what it feels like to live in this world. In fact, He went through that emotional week before Easter out of love for you. When we pray, we are sure that Jesus knows what we're going through. But Jesus didn't just experience suffering, did He? He also experienced joy and victory because He won over the sinful jeers, hurtful thoughts, death, and the devil. We can experience that joy with Jesus—here on earth and when we live with Him forever.

Journal:
How do you feel today? How does Jesus feel about you?

Pray:
Jesus, thank You for going through so much for me. Thank You for Your love. Amen.

L. C.

Revelation 22:20

Countdown

Ten . . . nine . . . eight . . . seven . . . What do you think about when you hear a countdown? Do you imagine a rocket launch? a New Year's Eve party? the last few moments before summer break?

When you think about it, the Bible is a little like a giant count-down. As soon as Adam and Eve sinned near the beginning of time, people have looked forward to the promise God gave in the Garden of Eden: a Savior would come to restore God's relationship with us. Ten . . . nine . . .

Abraham led his family to the land God promised and became a father to Isaac and eventually to nations—including the Messiah. Eight . . . seven . . .

Moses led God's people out of slavery and into the Promised Land, reminding us of our Deliverer. Six . . . five . . .

Esther pleaded for the life of the Jews—the people who would give the world the Redeemer. Four . . . three . . .

John the Baptist preached repentance and pointed to the coming Christ. Two . . . one . . .

As you look forward to Easter, remember that this was the point in history where God showed the world His salvation for all—through Jesus' death and resurrection.

With joy, we celebrate Easter. But we also remember that Jesus has promised to come again to bring all believers to Him forever. We start a new countdown—the countdown to the day when sin and death are no more! As we wait, let us tell others so that they may wait with us in joy and hope. Ten . . . nine . . . eight . . .

Journal:

Do you like waiting for things? What do you think it will be like when Jesus returns?

Pray:

God, thank You for keeping Your promise to save us through Jesus. Help me tell others this Good News of salvation as I wait for Jesus to come again. Amen.   L. C.

THURSDAY

Watch and Pray

"Ugh! There's just too much church this week!" Addyson was struggling with her socks while getting dressed. "Why do we even have so many services during such a busy time of the year? I'm tired of it."

Kristen, Addyson's teenage sister, was reading on the couch. "That sounds a little like this devotion," Kristen mentioned while turning a page. Addyson sidled up to her big sister.

"Oh, I remember that Bible passage," Addyson said. "The disciples kept falling asleep while Jesus was praying. If only they knew what was about to happen! If I was spending the evening with Jesus, I would definitely want to stay awake."

Kristen tried not to roll her eyes and smiled. "But that's exactly what we're doing tonight. Jesus promises to be with us when we gather in His name. We're hearing God's Word. And this is Maundy Thursday, when Jesus began the Lord's Supper. Jesus is present with us there too."

Addyson slipped on her shoe. "That's a good point. But I still have questions about Communion and how that works."

"Well," said Kristen as she closed her book, "it's a bit of a mystery for all of us, but I'm sure we'll learn more tonight. I'm just glad I can trust in Jesus' promises—like when He promises to be with us."

"Okay, I'll watch and pray tonight and learn more about Jesus and about Maundy Thursday," said Addyson. She added with a laugh, "It would be a shame to fall asleep!"

Journal:

Does spending time with Jesus sometimes seem tiring? What is helpful to remember when this happens?

Pray:

Lord, I'm sorry for not always paying attention to You and for "getting sleepy" when Your Word is near. Please forgive me and give me strength to learn more about You every day. Amen.   L. C.

LENT

5

6

7

8

9

LENT

| 10 | |

| 11 | |

| 12 | |

| 13 | |

| 14 | |

LENT

15

16

17

18

19

LENT

20

21

22

23

24

LENT

25

26

27

28

29

LENT

30	

31	

Drawings

40

My Devotions®

Daily Readings for Young Christians

Contributors to the April devotions:

Carol Albrecht, Eunice L. Graham, Edward Grube

Edited by Gail Pawlitz

VOL. 55　　　　MARCH–MAY 2013　　　　NO. 3

1 Romans 8:35–39

A Weird Easter Hunt

"This is weird," Sonia said to her brother, looking down at her Easter basket.

"Very weird," Joel agreed. "I wonder if Grandma is confused."

Sonia and Joel had been filling their Easter baskets with things their Grandma had hidden for them in her house. They had found several things hidden upstairs, but none of the treasures seemed to be Easter treats.

"Did you find everything?" Grandma called from downstairs.

"Yes, I think so, Grandma," Sonia called back. "But these treats seem a little strange."

"I guess they are different," Grandma replied. "Come downstairs, and I'll tell you why I chose them."

Sonia and Joel went downstairs. Joel pulled a big bag of chocolate hearts out of his basket. "Were these left over from Valentine's Day?" he asked.

"No," Grandma said. "Hearts are a symbol of love, and Easter is one of the best times to think about love."

"Why?" asked Sonia.

"Well, when Jesus died on the cross, it showed how much He loved us. If He had stayed dead, His love would just be in the past. Easter means that Jesus is alive now and forever. That means His love is forever. Jesus loves us right now, all the time, and we can always be sure of that. Easter means that Jesus' love is there for us every day."

"I never thought of it that way," said Joel. "These chocolate hearts make more sense to me now. Thanks, Grandma. I guess they are a sweet Easter treat, after all!"

Journal:

If you were to choose an Easter treat to help someone remember Jesus' love, what would it be?

Pray:

Dear Jesus, thank You for loving me today and every day. As I do my work today, guide my actions and words to reflect Your love. Amen.

E. L. G.

Bird Books

Sonia and Joel both liked bird-watching, especially in the woods behind Grandma's house. So they were happy to find pocket field guides among their Easter treats from Grandma. These guides had colorful drawings and descriptions of different birds they might see in the area.

"What about the bird books, Grandma?" Sonia said. "How do they remind us of Easter?"

"Well, do you ever see the birds gathering up food for the winter and storing it for themselves?" Grandma asked.

"No," said Joel. "If they stay in the colder areas during the winter, they find seeds to eat. Some people put out seeds and suet for them, like you do."

"And if they migrate, they go to a part of the world where there's food for them," Sonia added. "It's amazing how they know when to go and where to go and then how to come back."

They had been watching for returning birds in recent days. They were seeing lots of birds they hadn't seen all winter. The field guides would help them identify some of these birds.

"God takes amazing care of birds," Grandma said. "And Jesus promises that God loves us even more than He loves the birds. We can trust Him to take care of us. We can trust Him for our salvation through His gift of faith in Jesus."

"I get it," said Joel. "Because Jesus is alive, He cares for us every day. We don't have to worry about anything."

Journal:

What worries would you like to tell Jesus about? Write about them or about how the living Jesus cares for you.

Pray:

Dear Jesus, because You live, I can tell You all my worries and fears. This is a powerful truth. Help me remember this when I am troubled. Help me know You care about me and can help me. Amen.   E. L. G.

Sheep

Sonia and Joel each found a stuffed sheep among the treats Grandma had hidden for them. Sonia thought they were cute, but Joel thought they were silly-looking. He was catching on to Grandma's game, though. He thought he understood about the sheep.

"The sheep are to remind us that Jesus is our Good Shepherd, aren't they?" Joel asked.

"That's right," Grandma said. "Jesus said He is the Good Shepherd who laid down His life for His sheep."

"Sheep are another reminder that Jesus takes care of us, aren't they?" Sonia asked. "When Jesus said He is our Good Shepherd, that means He provides our food, water, and protection."

"Well, yes," said Grandma, "that's true, but there's something else I wanted you to remember. A shepherd leads his sheep, and they follow him. By ourselves, we don't know what to do or where to go in life. We need our Good Shepherd to lead us and guide us. Without Him, we'd soon get into trouble."

"I get into trouble anyway!" Sonia laughed. "But a shepherd brings back the sheep that don't follow him or those that get stuck in bad places."

"That's just what Jesus does for us," said Grandma. "We often sin and go away from Him, but He searches for us and is ready to forgive us. That's why we call Him our Good Shepherd. We can be happy that Jesus is alive to help and guide us, bringing us back and forgiving us when we sin."

"I think these sheep are kind of silly," Joel admitted, smiling. "But I like them. They are good reminders of how silly sheep can be, and that includes me! I'm glad that Jesus is my Good Shepherd."

Journal:
How does Jesus guide and lead you in your life?

Pray:
Dear Jesus, thank You for being my Good Shepherd. Please keep me close to You and lead me on to heaven. Amen.   E. L. G.

Revelation 21:3-4

Tissue Boxes

Maybe the weirdest things Sonia and Joel found in Grandma's Easter hunt were tissue boxes. Sonia's box was decorated with flowers. Joel's had a fancy gold design. Still, Sonia and Joel wouldn't have realized that these boxes were meant to be treats for them if there hadn't been sticky notes with their names attached.

Boxes of tissues are useful if you have a cold or if you are crying, but they didn't seem much like treats. Neither of them understood how the tissues could remind them of Easter. Sonia asked Grandma, "Why did you give us tissues?"

Grandma answered, "Through the years, many of my friends and family have died. I always feel sad, because I know how much I'll miss them. A box of tissues is handy when we need to cry about someone's death.

"There are other sad things that happen to us that make us cry. Easter is all about Jesus turning our tears into joy. He took our sadness away by rising from death to life again. We know He is alive and is always there to comfort us in our sadness. We can be sure that someday He will bring us to heaven, where there is no more sadness, no more death, no more crying.

"My favorite Easter hymn says, 'He lives to wipe away my tears.' That's how a box of tissues makes me think of Easter."

"I understand," said Joel. "We may not be happy all the time, but we know Jesus is alive and with us all the time."

"So when we're sad, He comforts us," Sonia added.

Journal:

In what ways does Jesus comfort us when we're sad? Is there someone you can share that comfort with right now?

Pray:

Dear Jesus, thank You for turning the sadness of death into the joy of Your resurrection. Please comfort me in times of sadness, until I am with You forever. Amen.   E. L. G.

THURSDAY

5

1 John 5:13–15

Pretzels

Grandma often made delicious homemade pretzels, and Sonia and Joel loved them. They were happy that Grandma included bags of her special pretzels on the Easter hunt. But even so, pretzels didn't seem like they belonged with Easter.

"I don't get it, Grandma," Joel said. "We sometimes have pretzels during Lent. We learned in Sunday School that a long time ago, pretzels were reminders to pray. They were given to children during Lent to remind them to say their prayers."

"Back when pretzels were first made, people crossed their arms on their chest to pray," Sonia added. "If you turn a pretzel upside down, it looks like arms crossed over your chest. That's why pretzels are prayer reminders."

"I'm glad you're both paying attention in Sunday School," Grandma said with a twinkle in her eye. "But should you pray only during Lent?"

"Of course not! We pray all year round!" Sonia answered.

"Easter is a good time to remember to pray. Because Jesus is alive, He hears our prayers all the time, every day and every night," Joel added.

"That's exactly right," said Grandma. "Jesus' resurrection is a comfort because it means He can hear and answer our prayers. If He has power over death, He also has power to help us with whatever we need. He's happy when we tell Him what's troubling us and also when we tell Him we love Him and thank Him for the good things He gives us. Easter means we have a living Savior to talk to!"

"I'm starting to see that everything good about being a Christian is all because of Easter!" Sonia said.

Journal:

Write a prayer thanking Jesus for hearing and helping you.

Pray:

Dear Jesus, thank You for always being there to hear and answer my prayers. Amen.   E. L. G.

Don't Be Afraid

"I love these candles you gave us, Grandma," Sonia said. "They are so pretty." Grandma had hidden candles decorated with small shells and beads for them to find on their Easter hunt.

"Are the candles supposed to remind us of the candles in church?" Joel asked.

"I suppose they could," Grandma answered. "I was actually remembering something else when I got these candles for you. Do you remember the time the power went out when you were little and were spending the night here with me? You were both so afraid in your dark bedroom by yourselves!"

"Yes, I remember," said Joel. "It was scary to be alone in the dark. Then you came to our room and told us not to be afraid. You lit some candles so it wouldn't be dark."

"I remember how scary it was," Sonia said. "The wind was howling outside, and branches were scratching on the windows."

"Jesus' disciples were afraid during a storm," Grandma reminded them. "But Jesus came to be with them and told them not to be afraid. When they knew He was with them, they weren't afraid anymore."

"So you gave us the candles to remind us not to be afraid," Sonia said.

"And because of Easter, we know Jesus is alive and so we never have to be afraid of anything," Joel added.

"Knowing that Jesus is alive is better than using a night-light!" said Sonia.

Journal:

What are some things that make you afraid? How can Jesus' resurrection give you courage?

Pray:

Dear Jesus, thank You for being with me all the time so that I know I don't ever have to be afraid of anything. Amen. E. L. G.

Angels

When Joel and Sonia found chocolate hearts during their Easter hunt, they thought Grandma had mixed up Valentine's Day with Easter. When they found angel ornaments, they wondered if perhaps she thought it was Christmas!

"These angels would look pretty on our Christmas tree," Sonia said to Grandma.

"Did you want us to remember the angels that were at the empty tomb on Easter morning?" Joel asked.

"Angels came from heaven to announce Jesus' resurrection," Grandma said. "I'm glad you remember that story. But what I wanted to remind you of is heaven, where God's angels praise Him. Because of what Jesus did on the cross for us, and because He rose from the dead, we can be sure that He will take us to heaven someday. That's the best news of Easter. If it weren't for Easter, there wouldn't be anything to look forward to after death. When we died, that would be the end. But now, we know we will live forever with Jesus in heaven."

"Easter is about our life now and about our life forever," said Joel. "All of the things you hid for us will help us remember that."

"This was the best Easter hunt ever!" Sonia said. "Thanks!"

"Can we do another one next year?" Joel asked. "Please, Grandma!"

"I know!" Sonia said. "Next year, we'll do an Easter hunt for *you*, Grandma! We'll see what we can think of to remind you of what Easter means!"

"That sounds like fun," Grandma agreed. "I'd enjoy that. But you know, I'll probably still have some treats for you!"

Journal:

What kinds of things would you hide on a special Easter hunt? What would they mean?

Pray:

Dear Jesus, thank You for giving me life now and forever through Your resurrection. Amen.   E. L. G.

2 Kings 5:10–11, 14

Meet Naaman

Naaman did not believe in the one true God. His young servant girl knew more about God than he did. Naaman's army had taken her from her people in Israel and forced her to work for Naaman's wife. Even so, she didn't forget that God loved her.

Naaman was sick with leprosy. The servant girl knew that God could cure leprosy. She told his wife that Naaman should visit a prophet in the land of Israel. By God's power, the prophet could heal him. Everyone was excited, even Naaman's king!

Naaman went to visit the prophet Elisha, but Elisha refused to see Naaman. Instead, Elisha sent a messenger to tell Naaman to dip himself seven times in the Jordan River. The messenger said, "Wash and be clean." This simple treatment was hard for Naaman to accept. Back home, Naaman was an important man. He traveled many miles to see Elisha for a cure. He brought lots of money to pay for the cure. And what happened? Elisha told him to go jump in the river! Naaman was angry. Some of Naaman's servants told him to do what the prophet said, even if it sounded silly. So Naaman dipped himself in the Jordan River. His leprosy disappeared!

This true story can help you think about what God did for sinners. He sent Jesus to die for sinners. Jesus was the only one who could cure people from sin. And what did sinners have to do? Jesus told them to be baptized. That's all! Then the Holy Spirit would begin His work.

We do not have to be important to be baptized. We do not have to pay for Baptism. Jesus did everything to take away our sins. Now He watches over us. He listens when we say we are sorry for our sins, and He forgives us. His Spirit is with us and helps us fight temptations to sin.

Journal:

Draw two pictures—one of Naaman dipping himself in the river and one of you getting baptized.

Pray:

Thank You, dear Jesus, for washing away my sins! Amen.   E. G.

MONDAY

1 Kings 3:7–9

Meet Solomon

How would you like to meet the wisest and richest king who ever lived? Some people think Solomon was that man. Solomon was chosen by God to lead God's people and care for them. To do that, he knew he needed God's help. He prayed the words of today's Bible reading and became an excellent king. Even other kings respected him.

Solomon shared his wisdom through proverbs—wise sayings. Many appear in the Bible book named Proverbs. Take some time later to read the first chapter of Proverbs.

Would you like to be like Solomon—rich and famous? What would you need to do to become like him?

Maybe better questions would be "How are you already like Solomon?" and "How did that happen?"

Okay, so you don't have lots of people wanting to hear how wise you are. You probably don't have stacks of gold and lots of servants either. Leaders from other countries haven't had the pleasure of hearing about you. Your parents and teachers may not always think you are very wise. In fact, they know you are a sinner, like they are. That's the bad news.

So, how are you like Solomon? You know the one true God. How do you know God? He gave you faith to believe in the triune God: Father, Son, and Holy Spirit. That faith came to you in Baptism and through His Word. Now, in Christ alone, you have salvation.

Solomon had lots of wisdom. You could trust him for advice. And you know the most important thing that he knew. You, too, have wisdom from God.

Journal:

Find the Book of Proverbs in your Bible. It is a collection of wise sayings from Solomon. Make up a wise saying you would like to share. Write a proverb for it.

Pray:

I praise You, dear God, for making me wise in faith. I know it is Your gift to me. Amen.   E. G.

10 Genesis 3:20

Meet Eve

Would you shake Eve's hand if you had the chance? Eve was first in lots of things. She was the first woman, the first wife, and the first sinner.

People would never forget her. Thousands of years later, people still remember Eve as the first sinner.

Eve and her husband, Adam, were also the first to hear God promise a Savior. God loved His first people so much—and all those who came after them—that He planned to save them from their sins. Many years later, God sent Jesus to die on a cross to take away Eve's sin—and the sins of everyone else, including you.

Eve is sometimes called the mother of all humans. Like a good mother, she taught us something important about sin and the devil.

If the devil came around looking like an ugly monster, you would know to be afraid. You would run away! But the devil doesn't come to us looking evil or dangerous.

The devil uses temptation. Most temptation looks like fun. As the devil, looking like one of Eve's animal friends, tempted her to disobey God, the devil tempts us too. The devil makes sin look like fun. The devil tempts us think that we don't need God's love or help. The devil wants us to disobey God by believing that Jesus is not our Savior—that He never really took away the sins of all sinners. We must be careful!

Like Eve, we know God's promise to do away with sin and defeat the devil. Jesus has taken away our sins. Someday, He will return and take us to live with Him in heaven.

Journal:

Write about the temptations you face. What makes them so tempting?

Pray:

Dear God, make me strong against temptation and the devil's lies, no matter how much fun it seems. I need Your help and forgiveness every day. In Jesus' name I pray. Amen.   E. G.

Revelation 1:9–10

Meet John

Does Jesus love you? You know He does. John knew it too. In fact, John was known as the disciple whom Jesus loved. Can you say the same?

Yes, you certainly can! John was not the only disciple whom Jesus loved. He loved them all. John, however, was very close to Jesus. You should know that you are very close to Jesus too.

Near the end of his life, John wrote about a vision he had when he was a prisoner on the island of Patmos. He was in prison because he talked about Jesus. He wanted everyone to know that Jesus lived and died and rose from the dead to take away their sins. Those who did not believe in Jesus thought they could stop John from talking about Jesus.

It didn't work. While John was on Patmos, God sent him visions. God showed John what it would be like to live in heaven. The last book of the Bible tells what John saw.

What do you know about heaven? The Bible does not give us a clear picture. Even Revelation, John's book, is full of mystery and hard-to-understand language.

God makes clear one thing about heaven: it is His home. Jesus and the Holy Spirit are there too. You will be there someday, along with all other believers.

Do you know why you will be in heaven? Is it because you try to be very good? Is it because you love Jesus? No, neither of those things are why you will go to heaven, though they may be true. The real reason is that God loved you so much that He sent Jesus to take away your sins. The Holy Spirit gave you the gift of faith to believe in Jesus. God did it all! You are a disciple whom Jesus loves.

Journal:

Write a note to your BFF that describes the best thing you know about heaven.

Pray:

Thank You, Jesus, for loving me and taking away my sins. Be with me until that day I meet You face-to-face in heaven. Amen.   E. G.

12 Luke 10:38

Meet Martha

You might think Martha goes to your church. She will be remembered as a hard worker. If you go to a church dinner, you might see lots of church members working hard to serve tasty food. Thank God for all those hard workers!

As long as you are meeting Martha, you should also meet her sister, Mary. They and their brother, Lazarus, were close friends of Jesus. When Jesus visited, Martha worked hard to make a delicious meal. Martha noticed that Mary didn't do much to help. She thought Mary was lazy, and she complained to Jesus.

Mary didn't help because she was listening to Jesus. She wanted to know more about her Savior.

Both Mary and Martha loved Jesus. They showed their love in different ways. Martha worked. Mary listened and learned. Who got more from Jesus' visit?

Working to please Jesus is important. Whatever good we do, we do because Jesus did everything good for us. Doing good for Jesus doesn't win us a place in heaven. God has already given us that.

Martha's sister, Mary, had a great idea. She wanted to know more about Jesus. She wanted to hear Him teach about God's work. She wanted to hear over and over how much Jesus loved her and all people.

Are you more like Martha, or are you more like Mary? Maybe you're a little bit like both. You go through these devotions, and you read Bible passages. You want to hear God's Word. After you hear God's Word, you want others to know His love. That is how you do good things for Him—by doing good things for others.

Journal:

Write three good things that you will do this week. Also write why you will do them.

Pray:

Dear Lord, make me like Mary—eager to hear Your Word. Make me like Martha too—eager to serve You. Amen.   E. G.

Meet Deborah

Deborah was smart. She was wise. She was tough. She was a singer. Deborah was a judge and prophetess who served God's people in Old Testament days.

Deborah's job was to help God's people make godly decisions. She also was to speak on behalf of God. He told Deborah to command a man named Barak to lead Israel's army against an enemy king named Sisera. Barak didn't think this was a good idea. He refused to lead the army unless Deborah came along.

Deborah agreed, and Barak's army defeated their enemy. God worked through Deborah and Barak to give His people victory. (You can read the entire exciting story in Judges 4:4–16.) After the battle, Deborah and Barak sang a victory song to praise God and tell the story of the battle. (You can read the song in Judges 5.)

This true story is one of many that tell how God always took care of His people. He used different ways and different people to do His work, but He always had one goal. He was preparing the world for the birth of Jesus. God's people—the group from which Jesus would someday be born—were often in trouble. Sometimes they caused their own trouble. Sometimes enemies from other nations caused trouble. God never let anything or anyone stop Him from sending Jesus to fight the biggest battle ever.

Jesus fought the devil. He didn't kill the devil, but He took away the devil's power over you and all believers. Easter, which we celebrated not long ago, is the celebration of Jesus' victory over the devil and death. Jesus' victory is truly something to sing about.

Journal:

Like Deborah, write a short song about Jesus and His victory, which saved you from death and the devil.

Pray:

Dear God, thank You for always taking care of Your people. I'm one of Your people too. Thank You for sending Jesus to save me. Amen.   E. G.

SATURDAY

14 Acts 15:36–38

Meet John Mark

John Mark might have had two names because that was the only way he would respond to his mother's call. Can you hear her? "John, please mow the lawn." No answer. "John Mark, get out there right now and mow the lawn!"

Okay, so that's probably not why he had two names. What we do know about John Mark is that he once was in trouble with the apostle Paul.

John Mark went with Paul on one of his missionary trips. Nobody knows what happened, but John Mark decided to leave Paul and return home. Paul was not happy about that. John Mark didn't turn out to be the kind of helper Paul wanted. It sounds as if he messed up.

Later, when Paul was about to travel again, he would not allow John Mark to go along. This was the consequence of whatever happened on the earlier trip. God gave John Mark another chance to travel on a different missionary trip.

God's workers make mistakes. Even the greatest names in the Bible—people such as Moses, David, Solomon, Martha—made mistakes in serving God. The great names suffered consequences of their sin too. But God never stopped loving them. God never quits on His people.

Do you mess up? Are you a sinner? Are you sometimes like John Mark? Do you avoid doing what you should do?

All God's people are like that, even the apostle Paul. Yet all sinners can have hope and peace. It comes from Jesus, who freed us from sin. Because Jesus lived, died, and rose from the dead to take away our sins, we are all forgiven. We all have another chance.

Journal:
Look back at all the Bible characters you met in last week's devotions. Who are you most like? In what ways?

Pray:
Thank You, dear Jesus, for taking away my sins. Help me to serve You well. Amen.   E. G.

Meet Job

Job is someone you should know. He was a family man. He and his wife had seven boys and three girls. The Bible says Job lived a good life. He loved God and hated sin. Job was rich too. Job lived such a happy and good life that the devil took a special interest in him.

The devil thought Job loved God and hated sin just because God blessed his life with so many earthly gifts. But God told the devil that Job would stay faithful no matter what happened. As you might imagine, the devil took this as a challenge. The devil made many terrible things happen to Job. All his children died! Job lost everything he owned too. His friends turned against him. To make matters worse, Job became very sick.

Job lost everything but his trust in God. Though he was sad and sick, Job said something that became the title of a famous Easter song. He said, "I know that my Redeemer lives, and at the last He will stand upon the earth. . . . I shall see God" (vv. 25–26). Job was sure that God was real and that He still loved Job.

Some people think God doesn't know what's happening when they are sick or when they lose their jobs or when life gets messed up in other ways.

Life is filled with sin. Aren't there times when you're treated badly or get sick? That is sin's way of messing up your life! But God doesn't let sin get in the way of His loving you. After all, He sent Jesus to take the punishment for your sins, and in His Word, He sends the Holy Spirit to make your faith stronger.

By the way, Job never lost faith, and God blessed him with an even better life than he had before! Your greatest life is yet to come too. Like Job, someday you will be in heaven with God.

Journal:

If you could make a word cloud to praise God, what words would you use? With permission, make one using a specialized Web site.

Pray:

Dear God, I know that my Redeemer, Jesus, lives. Thank You for giving me faith in Him. Please make it grow stronger every day. Amen.   E. G.

Meet Nehemiah

Nehemiah worked for a king, but he took on another job. He went into the remodeling business.

Nehemiah's hometown, Jerusalem, was in ruins. Once it had large walls to protect it, but an enemy had torn down the walls.

Nehemiah went back home. He was deeply saddened by what he saw. It was no easy job, but Nehemiah and his helpers rebuilt the wall.

Nehemiah also had an even more important remodeling job than rebuilding walls. He teamed up with a priest named Ezra to teach God's people how to worship God. They helped the people learn right from wrong, to confess their sins, and to receive God's forgiveness.

Do you know anyone in the business of remodeling? Some workers remodel houses. They make old rooms or old houses look new again. But what about people in the business of making life better?

Everyone's life needs remodeling because of sin. Sin troubles us through more than just the wrong things we do. Sin is the source of all sickness, wicked actions, and even death. Our sin-filled lives are like the crumpled walls of Jerusalem needing someone to repair them.

You know who has remodeled your life. It's Jesus Himself. He left His home in heaven to come to earth. His work on earth was to live a perfect life, suffer and die to pay for our sins, and come back to life in victory over sin and death.

We who know Jesus as our Savior are led by God's Spirit to confess our sins and receive God's gift of forgiveness. This wonderful gift rebuilds our life. It makes us new, just as if we had never sinned. Now we're ready to do what God wants us to do.

Journal:

Tell Jesus the wrong things (sins) you have done. Write what Jesus would say to you.

Pray:

Thank You, God, for telling me about Nehemiah. Thank You even more for telling me what Jesus did for me. Help me to tell others the Good News. Amen.   E. G.

Lamentations 3:21-24

Meet Jeremiah

Imagine this conversation with God's prophet long ago:

"How do you do? My name is Jeremiah. I didn't have much to laugh about during my days as a prophet. God's people didn't want to do what God wanted them to do. They were nasty and stubborn. God used me to teach them how to do what God wanted. I got beat up and tossed into a hole in the ground. It's almost too terrible to talk about.

"God was angry at His people because they were so bad. He punished them because He hoped that would help them behave more like His people. I wrote a group of poems in the Bible that go by the name of Lamentations. A lament is a sad saying.

"God told me to lament, but He also told me to share a little joy and happiness with the people. He never let me lose hope that the people would change. He was always ready to listen to His people say they were sorry for their sins. He was always ready to forgive them.

"And me? God gave me the honor and joy of writing some of the most beautiful words in the Bible, and they are in Lamentations! Please read them in today's Bible passage.

"I started by asking, 'How do you do?' Do you usually do what God wants of you—you know, obey the Ten Commandments and the like? To be honest, even though I worked for God, I wasn't perfect either. I could have written a lament about myself!

"God knows when we're sorry for our sins. And if you're like me, you're sorry a lot! But God will never let you down. Because Jesus suffered and died for your sins, He forgives you over and over and over and over. Great is God's faithful loving and caring for us!"

Journal:

Write a poem about how God is faithful to you. Don't make it a lament!

Pray:

I'm sorry for my sins, dear God. Please help me to hate sin and give me Your strength and power to be faithful to You. In Jesus' name I pray. Amen.

E. G.

18 Esther 4:13–14

Meet Esther

Have you ever been in the right place at the right time? Maybe you were by the table just when a child was about to spill his milk. Or maybe you were near when a parent needed help carrying a package.

Were you ever in the right place at the right time but were afraid to help? Or maybe you felt that you weren't able to help because the help needed was too great for you. That's how it was with Esther.

Esther became queen of Persia, even though she was not Persian. She was Jewish. Only God could make such a thing happen!

Some of the Persian people didn't like the Jewish people. They wanted to kill the Jews. To get the king of Persia to agree, they told lies about the Jews. Esther's uncle heard about the lies, so he told Esther that God's people were in danger. He wanted Esther to tell the king.

At first, Esther was afraid to tell the king. Even the queen didn't go talk to the king without being invited. If the king didn't like what the queen said, he could kill her! Esther had to risk death. God had placed her in the right place at the right time to save her people. What would she do?

God gave Esther courage to do the right thing. Instead of being angry with Esther, the king became angry at some of his own people. He had them arrested and killed for their plot against Esther's people.

At just the right time God had a job for Esther. At just the right time, Jesus came to earth to save God's people. Jesus paid for our sins with His own suffering and death on the cross. He saved God's people.

At just the right time, we'll meet Jesus and God the Father and the Holy Spirit—and Esther too. Once again, we'll be in the right place at the right time, and what a joyous time that will be!

Journal:
Draw a time when God was in the right place protecting you.

Pray:
Dear Jesus, You have saved me through Your perfect sacrifice. Through Your Spirit, send me today to do the good You have planned for me. Amen.   E. G.

Luke 19:1–10

Meet Zacchaeus

Zacchaeus: you either love him or hate him. He may be like someone in your class. In Jesus' day, most people hated him, and he gave them plenty of reasons.

Zacchaeus collected taxes for the government. In itself, that wasn't a bad job; somebody had to do it. The problem came when Zacchaeus collected more taxes than what people owed. He kept the extra for himself. He probably had several other bad habits too.

Lots of important people were in the crowd one day waiting to see Jesus. Zacchaeus was too short to see over the crowd, so he climbed a tree. Many people in the crowd thought they were good. They fooled themselves into thinking they obeyed all of God's laws. Many people thought they were better than Zacchaeus. Many people thought Jesus should pay attention to them.

Jesus surprised them. Jesus saw Zacchaeus up in the tree. He told Zacchaeus to come down. They were going to have lunch together! The crowd was angry. They didn't think Jesus should eat with a cheating tax collector!

The great thing about Jesus is that He came to save sinners. Jesus wanted to know sinners like Zacchaeus. He wanted sinners to know Him.

Jesus wants to be with you too. You might not be as sinful as Zacchaeus—you might be worse! It doesn't matter. Jesus wants to be with you. In His Word and in Baptism, He promises to be with you and forgive you. He died to take the punishment for your sins. He listens when you say you're sorry for your sins and forgives you. He gives you power to resist sin.

Journal:

Zacchaeus climbed a tree to get a better look at Jesus. Write about where you would go to get a better look at Jesus.

Pray:

Lord Jesus, thank You for coming to save sinners. Thank You for coming to save me. Help me to learn more about You as I read the Bible. Amen.

E. G.

SATURDAY

Meet Luke

Luke was different from Jesus' first group of disciples. He wasn't an eyewitness to Jesus' life as were Matthew, Mark, and John. Instead, Luke studied information about Jesus and then told His story. God used Luke's skill in his work—Luke was a doctor—to tell what Jesus did for us.

Luke wrote about Jesus' love for all people. God wants all kinds of people to know Jesus as their Savior. And He wants all kinds of people to tell others about Jesus too.

Luke lived an exciting and sometimes dangerous life. As a doctor, he could have lived in comfort, but God wanted Luke to work with the famous apostle Paul. He traveled with Paul to many places where Paul did missionary work. This gave Luke a chance to write about the spread of the Christian faith in the years after Jesus returned to heaven. Luke wrote this history in the Bible book known as Acts.

Since you are a sinner, Luke wrote his book for you. The Holy Spirit worked through Luke to tell the Good News to sinners. He wrote about the birth, teachings, death, and resurrection of Jesus.

When you confess your sins, you can be sure that Jesus forgives you. You know this because the Holy Spirit has given you faith to believe that Jesus is your Savior. You also know this because God's Word is true. In books such as Luke's, it tells you so.

Luke wrote about prayer too. He reported that Jesus Himself prayed, especially before something important was about to happen. Jesus wants you to pray too. You don't have to worry about how important the thing is that you're praying about. Jesus is always willing to listen.

Journal:

If you had Luke's job of writing about Jesus, write the three most important things you would say.

Pray:

Dear God, thank You for giving us people like Luke to tell us the true story of Jesus. Thank You even more for sending Jesus to take away our sins. In His name I pray. Amen.   E. G.

Meet Jael

Have you ever met a hero? Have you ever met a hero hardly anyone knows? Well, meet Jael.

Jael is famous—okay, almost famous—because she killed a wicked king whose name was Sisera. This king was mean to God's people, and he was powerful enough to get away with treating them badly. God's people complained about Sisera and asked God to help them.

You never know whom God will use to do His work. God's workers do the work God wants them to do. In the past week, you read what God wanted some of His workers to do. For Nehemiah, it was rebuilding a wall. For Esther, it was telling the king about a plot to kill her people. For Luke, it was writing down the history of Jesus and the first Christians. What is God's job for you?

Right now, you have many different jobs. Sometimes we call those jobs "vocations." You are a son or daughter. Maybe you are a brother or sister. You might be a runner on the track team, or you might play the clarinet. You might be a Girl Scout or Boy Scout, a pianist or gymnast. You probably have a job being a good friend or neighbor. I doubt that God is asking you to do what Jael did to help her country, but God has other important things for you to do today.

Jesus' perfect payment for your sin makes Him better than a hero. He is your Savior. And by His grace, every day is an adventure for you. With the new life God has given you in Baptism, you are free from trying to save yourself—something you could never do. You are free to serve others. To help, God works inside you.

When you work in your vocations, God works. He gives you ways to speak about your Savior, Jesus. He gives you time to show forgiveness and love to others. He gives you an adventure with Him.

Journal:

Make a list of all your vocations. Ask God to bless you in each one.

Pray:

Dear God, thank You for using people to work in Your kingdom. Give me a gentle spirit and many opportunities to speak and show Your love. Amen.   E. G.

MONDAY

Bless You!

The next devotions are about some ways in which you are blessed. The Bible readings are from a part of the Bible called the Beatitudes. Jesus wanted to explain the blessings that Christians have because of their faith in Him.

Your first blessing might not sound like a blessing, but here it is anyway: "Blessed are the poor in spirit, for theirs is the kingdom of heaven."

You may not think of yourself as being poor in spirit, but you are. Let's spend a little time getting to understand this blessing.

Ask yourself these questions:

Do I agree that I do wrong things (sin)?

Am I sorry for the wrong things I do?

If you answered yes, then you are poor in spirit. But being poor in spirit sounds so unhappy, doesn't it?

You know about your sins, and the Holy Spirit makes you sorry for your sins. You also know what Jesus did to your sins, right? He took them to the cross and paid the punishment you deserved because of them. As you probably know, Jesus didn't remain dead after dying on the cross and being placed in a grave. He came back to life!

In Baptism, God washed away your sins. In Baptism, the Holy Spirit gave you the gift of faith, and you became a member of God's kingdom. Even though you still live on earth, you live in God's kingdom right now. Someday, Jesus will return to end the world. When that happens, you and all believers will come alive for a new and never-ending life in the part of God's kingdom called heaven.

Journal:

Now that you know what "poor in spirit" means, draw a cartoon that shows you acting out what it's like to be poor in spirit.

Pray:

Thank You, dear Jesus, for taking away my sins. Through the power of Your Holy Spirit, give me power to fight sin as I look forward to that day when I meet You face-to-face. Amen.   E. G.

How Sad

Name a few things that make you sad. Really sad. Not sad like when you miss your favorite TV show. Not sad like when you lose your baseball game. But really sad like when a bad storm knocks down some houses.

As long as you're being sad, how do you feel about Jesus' suffering and death for your sins? Now, that's sad!

Our beatitude for today says, "Blessed are those who mourn, for they shall be comforted." People who mourn show their sadness. They might cry, and you can hear the sadness in their voices. One of your blessings is that you mourn. Is this really a blessing?

It is a blessing to know where sadness comes from. Bad things do not come from God. They come from sin and the devil. How sad when we think about the bad things that have happened to the world that God created to be good! We can blame the devil for much of the sadness in the world, but the devil doesn't make us do wrong. We do it ourselves. And our own sin can make us sad.

We can't stay sad for long. Why?

Today's blessing says that we will be comforted. God has good news for us. He can make us feel better even when things around us are sad. God's promises can cheer us up when we are sad about our own sins. Going from sad to happy is a good thing!

God already made something good happen. Your sins are forgiven. Jesus took them away. Someday, even more good will happen. Everything that makes us sad will go away. Jesus will take us to heaven. Can you just imagine the happy party we'll have when we get there? It will last forever.

Journal:

Write what makes you sad. Then use a dark marker to cross out all your words. Someday, all those sad things will be gone!

Pray:

Comfort me, dear God. So many things make me sad. Help me remember that my sins are forgiven and that Jesus will come again. Then I'll be happy forever. In Jesus' name I pray. Amen.   E. G.

T
U
E
S
D
A
Y

24 Matthew 5:5

Who Gets What?

Bullies can come in any size. Marcus had everything a bully needs to be an outstanding bully. He was tall. He had huge muscles. He never smiled. He even had a little bit of hair growing above his upper lip. He was especially good at breaking the Second, Fifth, Seventh, and Eighth Commandments. Marcus always got what he wanted.

Marcus would probably laugh at the third beatitude: "Blessed are the meek, for they shall inherit the earth." One of your blessings is that you are meek.

Meek people are not bullies, but they are strong. They have strength that God gives them. They are strong in hidden ways.

You might think meek people don't get much of anything that is good. You might think that meek means the same thing as weak. A bully would call a meek person a wimp—or maybe something worse! (Hmm. Maybe you want to think about accepting the blessing of being meek.)

Jesus said that you "shall inherit the earth." Jesus meant that you and all Christians will end up with every good thing. What do you think is the best thing you could have?

Life with Jesus might be at the top of your list. When you're with Jesus, you won't need to worry about bullies—even if you meet Marcus in heaven. Marcus in heaven? Bullies go to heaven? Yes, God forgives bullies. In heaven, they won't be bullies anymore because they, too, will be blessed with meekness.

The idea of Marcus in heaven is okay with believers who already are blessed with meekness. They know God's forgiveness is for all sinners because Jesus died to take away all the sins of all people.

Journal:

Draw what you think meek Marcus and meek you and meek Jesus might someday do together in heaven.

Pray:

Dear Jesus, help me to forgive others as You forgive them. Help me to forgive just as You forgive me. Thank You for blessing me with meekness. Amen.

E. G.

Matthew 5:6

Good Food

What kind of food do you want when you're hungry?

If you are really, *really* hungry, most any food is probably okay. Sometimes you're hungry for only one kind of food, right? Even if you aren't hungry, do you agree that you need food to stay alive?

Today's beatitude says, "Blessed are those who hunger and thirst for righteousness, for they shall be satisfied."

Have you ever tasted righteousness? It's not in any of the food groups you've learned about in school. You can't bake it for an hour. It doesn't taste like chicken. It tastes more like a picture word!

Jesus often used picture words to help His disciples understand what He was teaching. When He talked about the blessing of hunger for righteousness, He was saying that God's people want to please Him—it's like they are hungry to make God happy. There is only one way to do this—and you already have it: you have to be perfect!

Okay, so maybe you think of yourself as only very good. You are wrong. When Jesus suffered, died, and came alive again to take away your sins and beat the devil, He made you perfect in God's sight. When God looks at you, He doesn't see your sins. He sees a forgiven sinner—a perfectly forgiven child of God because of Jesus.

Okay again. So you know you're not perfect, and that probably bothers you. When you feel this way, you're feeling hunger for righteousness! You want to be in the right shape in front of God. This blessing keeps you close to God, because you know that each time you ask forgiveness for your wrongness, God sees what Jesus did for you: He made you righteous.

Journal:

Write a three- or four-line poem that tells how you became righteous.

Pray:

Dear Jesus, thank You for making me righteous in God's sight and for blessing me in Baptism. Help me rejoice, live in Your forgiveness, and hunger for righteousness. Amen.   E. G.

F
R
I
D
A
Y

Say "Uncle"

Most of the time, Mandy's brother was nice. He helped her with homework and told her jokes. He liked to tickle her too. Mandy didn't like *too* much tickling because she would laugh but then begin to cry. Her brother wouldn't stop tickling her until she said "uncle." Saying "uncle" was like saying, "You win. Now please leave me alone."

One day, Mandy wanted to teach her brother a lesson. She sneaked up behind him and began tickling him. He laughed until he fell off the chair. He laughed and laughed and laughed. Suddenly, Mandy stopped tickling him. She didn't make him say "uncle" or make him beg her to stop. She had mercy on him.

Mercy is getting what you don't deserve. Another way to say it is that you don't get what you do deserve! Mandy could have tickled her brother until he cried. Instead, she showed mercy.

Today's beatitude says, "Blessed are the merciful, for they shall receive mercy." Because you belong to Jesus' family, you are blessed with mercy. God gives you mercy even though you deserve to be punished for your sins. God knew what you needed, so He sent Jesus to pay for your sins—to take the punishment you deserved. Now you are blessed also to give mercy.

Everyone needs mercy. Think of ways you might show mercy to others even if they don't deserve it. God blesses His people with many opportunities.

Isn't it great to be so blessed? So far, you've read about five ways God blesses you. By the time you read Sunday's devotion, you'll learn two more.

Journal:

God blessed you with mercy. How has someone shown mercy to you?

Pray:

Dear God, You had mercy on me. In the name of Jesus, give me Your power and love to have mercy on others, especially those in my family. Amen.
                                                                    E. G.

Matthew 5:8

Ready to See God

People get cleaned up when they go to see somebody important. When do you get cleaned up? Is it to visit the doctor? to visit Grandma or Grandpa? What if you were going to see God?

Someday, you will see God! He wants you to live with Him. Of course, if you want to see God, you will need to be clean. How will you ever be clean enough?

You can wash your face, scrub your elbows, shampoo your hair, and scrape the dirt from under your fingernails. That's all good, but it will not make you clean enough to see God.

You know a person can look really good on the outside and still be mean and nasty on the inside. God knows that too, so He looks to see if people are clean on the inside. You cannot be clean on the inside unless you have no sin. Who can be that clean?

You can! Do you remember all the ways God has blessed you? Here is another: "Blessed are the pure in heart, for they shall see God." God has blessed you with a pure heart. It was His gift in Baptism. You know how a person gets gifts. Someone must buy them. Your pure heart came from Jesus. He gave His life to pay for your pure heart. When He died on the cross, the debt was paid.

What do you think your friends might answer if you asked, "How will you be ready to see God?" They might talk about obeying parents and teachers. Maybe they will say that going to church every week or praying before bedtime will make them ready to see God. You may hear nothing about a pure heart. They need to know that they can do nothing to get a pure heart. They need to know that a pure heart is God's gift. He blesses all who believe in Jesus with a pure heart.

Journal:

Write a note to God. Tell Him you're ready to see Him anytime He wants. Tell Him why you're ready.

Pray:

Thank You, dear Jesus, for taking away the sins that made me unclean and for making me ready to see God through Your death and resurrection. Amen. E. G.

Peace

Is Sunday one of your favorite days? Many people like Sunday because that day gives them peace. Maybe they can sleep later. They might have extra time to read the newspaper before going to church. They may take the afternoon to nap, visit others, or do nothing.

God's peace is different from all other kinds of peace. His peace takes work. Today's beatitude says, "Blessed are the peacemakers, for they shall be called sons of God."

Did you notice the difference between the words *peace* and *peacemaker*? *Peacemaker* suggests that peace is possible only when people *make* peace. Thank and praise God! He sent the Prince of Peace to make peace between sinners and Himself.

You are blessed to have Jesus as your peacemaker because God is at war against sin. You have to admit that you sin often, right? Jesus earned peace with God for you. You have read enough devotions like this to know how Jesus did it. God's Word tells us that He beat sin to death when He died on the cross and came alive again on the first Easter. Jesus was the peacemaker who gave you peace with God. He did it by forgiving your sins.

You can't make peace as well as Jesus did, but you can use your blessing to try some peacemaking. When God helps you forgive others, you share His peace. Your model is the Prince of Peace—Jesus Himself!

Your blessing of peace is not like other kinds of peace. Two friends might argue and then find peace with each other. Often the peace does not last because they argue again. Your peace with God isn't like that. Your Prince of Peace made peace between you and God on Sunday and forever.

Journal:

The dove is the picture we use to think about the Holy Spirit. Draw one. If you need some help, first check out an Internet picture.

Pray:

Dear Prince of Peace, through the power of Your Holy Spirit, give me Your power to be a peacemaker. Amen.　　　　　　　　　　　E. G.

1 Corinthians 15:3–6

Just the Facts, Please!

Did you know that a hard-boiled egg will spin? An uncooked or soft-boiled egg will not. Were you aware that the kiwi bird of New Zealand has a nostril at the end of its beak and finds food by smell? Did you know buttermilk does not contain any butter?

You might be surprised to learn that the famous physicist Albert Einstein never wore any socks. And his favorite pastime was sailing. Although he won the Nobel Prize in physics, he wasn't present to accept it. Instead, he was on a voyage to Japan.

Facts can be surprising, interesting, and even funny. But one thing we know about all of them—if they are facts, they have to be true.

Paul gives us some interesting facts in today's Bible reading. He doesn't say, "I think Christ died for our sins" or "Maybe He was raised on the third day." What Paul says is fact: "Christ died for our sins. . . . He was raised on the third day" (vv. 3–4). Those things really happened.

The fact that Jesus died and rose again is wonderful news. It is a fact that He gave His life for us. It is a fact that He rose again. And it is a fact that those who believe in Jesus have their sins forgiven. It is a fact that they will spend eternity in heaven with their Savior.

This world is full of interesting facts. But only the truths of Jesus' death and resurrection can save us. And in Baptism and through God's Word, we have faith to believe the most wonderful facts of all!

Journal:

Why is it so important to know Jesus' death and resurrection are facts and not fiction?

Pray:

Lord, I am happy that You really lived, died, and rose again. Thank You for the faith to believe the facts in the Bible. Help me share the facts of Your Word with others. Amen.   C. A.

TUESDAY

Real Beauty

"I can't wait for Saturday, Bridgett, when you come over," exclaimed Darnae. "Marcy is coming too. She's beautiful. You'll like her."

On Saturday, Bridgett was a little nervous. If Marcy was so pretty, she thought, she might be stuck up and no fun. Bridgett looked for Marcy when she walked in. There was no one there but a girl in a wheelchair. Her legs seemed too small for her body, and one arm hung limply. She wore thick glasses and had a brace on her neck.

"Hi, Bridgett. I'm Marcy," said the girl. "I'm glad to meet you. I brought along a game. It will be fun with three people."

The girls played together all afternoon. Marcy made them laugh with the funny things she said. She was one of the nicest people Bridgett had ever met. When Bridgett left, she whispered to Darnae, "Marcy really is beautiful!"

Bridgett learned something important that day—beauty isn't on the outside but on the inside. The prophet Samuel learned that too. God wouldn't let Samuel pick a king because he was handsome. Instead, God told him, "the LORD looks on the heart" (v. 7).

God also looks at our hearts, where ugly sin lives. But He sent Jesus to die so that our ugly, sinful hearts could become beautiful. He gives us the Holy Spirit. He beautifies our hearts through faith. With the Spirit in our hearts, they become beautiful in God's eyes.

God led Samuel to choose David as king. He became one of the greatest kings of Israel. David believed in the Savior to come. He loved the Lord. Through faith in the coming Savior, God made David's heart beautiful. He does the same for us so that we, too, can shine from the inside out.

Journal:

Explain in your own words what makes someone "beautiful." Are you beautiful in God's eyes? Why?

Pray:

Thank You, Jesus, for dying for me. Thank You for forgiving my sins and making me beautiful. Amen. C. A.

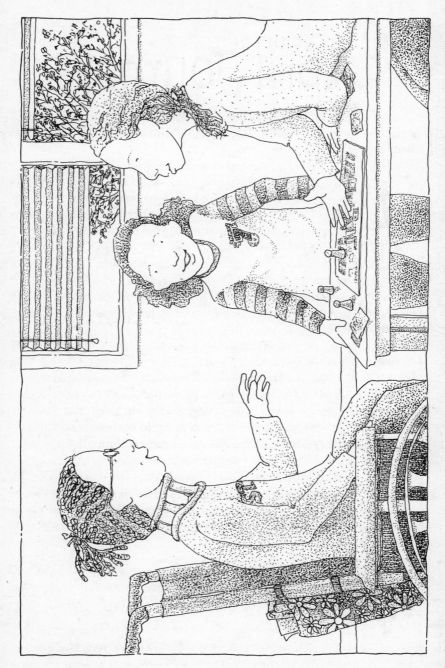

April Journal

1

2

3

4

Christ is risen! Alleluia!

5

6

7

8

9

Christ is risen! Alleluia!

10

11

12

13

14

Christ is risen! Alleluia!

15

16

17

18

19

Christ is risen! Alleluia!

20	

21	

22	

23	

24	

Christ is risen! Alleluia!

25

26

27

28

29

Christic is risen! Alleluia!

30

Drawings

My Devotions®

Daily Readings for Young Christians

Contributors to the May devotions:

Julie Dietrich, Cheryl Honoree, Phil Lang,
Gloria Lessman, Lacy Marsh, Malinda Walz

Edited by Gail Pawlitz

VOL. 55   MARCH–MAY 2013   NO. 3

1

Galatians 5:22–23

May Day

Have you ever knocked on someone's front door, hung a basket of treats or flowers on the handle, and yelled "May Day" as you ran away to a hiding place?

In the little Nebraska town where I grew up, that's what we all did on May 1. From our hiding places, we watched to see what would happen. Usually, the door opened, and our friends looked around and soon spotted the May basket filled with goodies hanging there. May Day was a fun springtime celebration, one we welcomed along with the daffodils.

In spring, we also welcomed the arrival of gentle rains and green leaves on bare branches. New shoots emerged from bulbs. New life sprang from dormant roots. God gave life to spring.

Sadly, we can't make new life spring forth in us. We were born in sin, born dead. Have you noticed how easy it is to get upset with your friends, to lie just a little, to disobey your parents, to become proud or mean-spirited? That's what is natural for us.

Then came Jesus. He suffered and died for us. He rose from the grave. He offers His new-life gifts to us. In Baptism and through His Word, His Spirit comes to give us faith so that we receive new life.

That new life spouts and blossoms in love, joy, peace, patience, kindness, goodness, gentleness, and self-control. With God's help, we now have the ability to forgive our friends, to tell the truth, to obey gladly, and to be humble. Those are the new-life gifts we can share with our family and friends today and every day.

Journal:
Draw a May basket. Fill it with words that identify the fruit of the Spirit you read about in Galatians 5.

Pray:
Thank You, Holy Spirit, for giving me new life and new ways to live because of what Jesus has done for me. Amen.   P. L.

John 3:16

A Puzzle for You

Solve the puzzle that follows to find out why God sent His Son to die for you. Cross out the letters X, B, and Z.

X	B	F	O	R	B	X	G	O	D
X	Z	S	O	L	B	O	Z	V	E
Z	D	X	B	Y	O	U	X	T	H
A	T	X	B	H	E	X	B	D	I
E	D	Z	Z	X	F	B	O	X	R
X	X	Y	O	U	X	Z	B	X	Z

Did you find out why God sent His Son? Because God loved you!

An important church leader named Nicodemus was puzzled by Jesus' actions and teachings, so he came one night to chat with Jesus. Nicodemus and Jesus talked about how a person becomes part of God's kingdom and how someone old can be born again.

You know how it happens, right? It happens through the power of Baptism. Through Baptism, a person of any age is born again through water and the Spirit. There, a baby, toddler, tween, teen, or adult becomes a child in the kingdom of God.

Someday, some puzzled person may ask you, "What do I have to do to be born again?" You know the answer: you don't do anything. God does it all. In love, He sent His Son, Jesus, to die for your sins. In love, He gives you faith. In love, He forgives your sins and gives you eternal life. Now the puzzle is what would you like to do?

Journal:

If you, like Nicodemus, could sit down and chat with Jesus, what would you ask Him?

Pray:

Dear Jesus, thank You for loving me so much that You came down to earth to be human like me in order to save me! Help me to share this great news with others. Amen.   P. L.

Psalm 37:1–7

FRIDAY

Fret Not

It had been a rough day for Isaiah. Someone stole his new bike from the rack at school. Not even the crossing guard could figure out where it was or who had taken it. The police were checking.

Isaiah stared at the wall and quietly prayed. His brother, Isaac, tried to lighten the mood. "Let's do something fun, Isaiah," he said. "I know you feel bad."

Isaiah looked up. "It's just not fair!" he said. "I did everything right. I locked up my bike right where I always do. Mom and Dad can't afford to buy me a new bike. And I don't have enough money saved up. What are we going to do?"

"We're going to trust God, Isaiah. So now, let's do that and play some ball," said Isaac. "I'll hit you grounders. Hey, maybe Dad would like to play. I think I hear him coming up the steps."

Just then Dad appeared in the doorway. "Did I hear someone say baseball?" he asked. "Let me change my clothes. I'll be right there."

"Wait, Dad," Isaiah blurted. "Did you hear about my bike? It's awful, isn't it? What are we going to do?"

Dad turned around. "I'm sorry, Son. I should have said something. Your mom called me and told me someone stole your bike. She said the police are looking for it. We'll trust in the Lord for a solution. I do know God doesn't want us to fret about it.

"We can't replace your bike right away, but we can trust that evil hasn't won. God is going to take care of us, right? Through Jesus' suffering and death, He overcame all evil. Isaiah, you are God's child, and He won't abandon you or Isaac or your mom or me. Not ever. Now, let's play some ball."

Journal:

Choose your favorite verse from Psalm 37. Use colorful markers to write it in your journal.

Pray:

Dear Jesus, help me to "fret not" when it seems evil is winning. Instead, lead me to trust in Your care, now and always. Amen.   P. L.

Mark 1:16–20

Follow Jesus

Can you imagine Jesus sitting behind the steering wheel of a van, driving the disciples around Jerusalem on a tour? Of course not. Jesus did not drive a car. He did not ride on a bus, train, or airplane. He did not own a bicycle, skateboard, or scooter. Everywhere Jesus went, He walked. Often, people followed Him.

Jesus wants lots of followers. When He first began His ministry, He walked by a seashore. He called James and John to leave their nets and follow Him. Later, He invited other men—people like Matthew, Bartholomew, and Philip—to be His disciples and follow Him.

So the disciples walked too, following Jesus. They walked to Jericho and Jerusalem, to Samaria and Caesarea. They walked to many places where Jesus did miracles, explained the kingdom of God, and trained His disciples to be His witnesses. Jesus was teaching everyone how to follow Him by faith.

One sad day, Jesus walked up to Calvary. There, His feet stopped, and soldiers nailed them to a cross. After a few hours, Jesus died for the sins of all people. Then Jesus' followers wrapped His body and placed it in a grave.

Was this the end of following Jesus? Certainly not! It was just the beginning, because Jesus did not stay dead. He rose victorious. And because He lives, we will too.

Now we walk by faith, faith that the Holy Spirit gives us. Yes, that's how we follow Jesus. We trust in Him for our salvation. We leave our "Jesus footprints" wherever we go—at home, at school, and in the big, wide world of our neighborhoods.

What do Jesus' footprints look like? They look like yours.

Journal:

Draw a footprint in your journal. Inside it, write down the places you and God will go today.

Pray:

Dear Jesus, by Your Spirit, keep me faithful. Help me walk each day as a child of God, trusting in Your mercy and sharing Your love. Amen. P. L.

Mark 15:16–20; 16:19–20

Bad or Good

Millie walked slowly into the house after playing soccer. She wandered over to Mom. "My tummy hurts!" she moaned.

Mom stopped putting away dishes and wrapped her arm around Millie. "I'm sorry, Sweetie," she said gently. "Maybe you should sit and read for a while. Then you and your tummy can rest." Millie agreed. She picked up her mystery and sat in her favorite chair.

It wasn't long until her brother came limping into the house and called out for his mom. She put down the towel once again. "Oh, dear! What happened?" she asked.

Alex limped closer. "I stepped on Jose's foot."

Mom checked the swelling. "It looks like you twisted your ankle," she said. "It must hurt. How about sitting in the living room while I get an ice pack?"

Alex and Millie were both in pain. They didn't think pain was good. What do you think? Is pain good or bad? No one really likes pain. It hurts. So in that way, pain is bad. But pain lets you know something is wrong so you can rest your body and heal. So in that way, pain is good.

The Bible tells us that Jesus was arrested, mocked, whipped, and nailed to a cross. Jesus endured a lot of pain, on purpose. And that was bad, but His death for our sins was also good. Through His suffering and death, Jesus paid the price for our sins, something we could never do. So Jesus made it possible for us to be God's children and live forever with Him. That's really good.

Journal:

Jesus endured pain and suffering so you could be His child and live forever with Him. Think back over your life. Has anyone in your family ever suffered something for your good? If you think of something, write about it.

Pray:

Dear Jesus, thank You for suffering all that bad pain so I could be a child of God and live forever with You. Amen.   P. L.

M O N D A Y

A River, a Well, and a Spring

I live near an unusual stretch of the Santa Ana River. Instead of the river being filled with water, it is usually filled with sand, lots of sand. At times, bulldozers move the sand around to make little walls, or berms. Because we don't get much rain, the Anaheim Water District built a dam and reservoir to store up the river water instead of letting it go downstream to the ocean.

Periodically, they release the water from the reservoir to fill the "sandboxes." That water slowly percolates through the sand and soaks into the ground below. That way, the city has more water underground to pump up during a dry spell. It's a great way to conserve and recycle water!

Some people, like those of us in Anaheim, use city water, and some people get their water from wells. However we get water, one thing is sure: we all need water to live. We can't survive more than three days without it.

One day, Jesus was thirsty. He stopped by a well near Sychar and asked a woman for some water. While He was there, He taught her about living water that could spring up in her and give her eternal life. He said, "Everyone who drinks of this water [meaning the well water] will be thirsty again, but whoever drinks of the water that I will give him will never be thirsty again. The water that I will give him will become in him a spring of water welling up to eternal life."

Jesus gives the water we need for eternal life, for forgiveness and salvation. He is the only way we can live forever. And because we are God's children, His Spirit makes good things spring up in us.

Journal

Imagine a spring of good things coming from you. Write about the good things Jesus has given you.

Pray:

Dear Jesus, I confess that sin makes me thirsty for You and the forgiveness only You can provide. Fill me with Your water of eternal life. Amen.

P. L.

Ephesians 6:14

Is Your Heart Covered?

Years ago, an armored soldier wore a breastplate on the chest to cover his heart. Because the heart is the life-giving organ of the body, covering it was a matter of life and death. No soldier would fight without it. Today, soldiers and police officers wear bullet-proof vests for the very same reason.

We are God's armored soldiers and need to cover our hearts. Every day, we battle against sneaky sin, scary death, and the pesky devil. This struggle isn't new to us; it's been around since the beginning of time. Because Adam and Eve sinned in the Garden of Eden, the hearts of all people from that time on are sinful. Not only do we have this sinful condition, but we think, say, and do sinful things. Even when we try to be on our best behavior, we fail. There is no way to be perfect. We have no righteousness of our own.

To fill our need for righteousness, God joined the battle. He gives us Christ's righteousness, and it becomes our breastplate. Paul tells us in 2 Corinthians 5:21 that God made Jesus, His perfect Son, to be our sin. Jesus died to pay for every sin, and then He rose from the dead so that we could be righteous (all right). Jesus covers our sinful hearts and deeds with His perfect "right-ness." His "breastplate of righteousness" guarantees that our sins cannot get us down. Death cannot win over us. The devil cannot accuse us before God.

Is your heart covered? Sure it is—with Jesus' righteousness.

Journal:
Draw a big heart. Inside it write "Jesus makes me right with God."

Pray:
Lord God, You have redeemed me. Thank You for sending Your perfect Son to live the righteous life I cannot live. Give me joy in Your forgiveness and opportunities to serve others in Your name. For Jesus' sake I pray. Amen.   G. L.

8 Ephesians 5:19–20

The Songs Stuck in You

"La, la, la!"

Have you ever had a song's melody and lyrics stuck in your head? Catchy tunes can play over and over in us like we have an internal radio. Pretty soon, we're singing out loud and tapping our feet.

When the lyrics are helpful, uplift others, or give God praise, we glorify God. That's great. But what if the lyrics are bad? What if we listen to things that displease God? If we hear others complaining, saying bad words, or discussing inappropriate topics, those things get stuck in our minds. That filthy or foolish talk might even come from us, from our sinful nature. When that happens, God's children need to repent. We need God's mercy. So it's good to know God is waiting to take away our bad-song burdens and forgive our sins.

The song of God's children reflects our new life in Christ. Now how does that song get stuck in us? It comes from God's Spirit, who in Baptism and through God's Word puts new life us. With that life comes no ordinary tune!

When we read the Bible, we hear God's voice. We hear how He loved us. He sent His only Son to die for our sins, and He rose victorious on Easter. Alleluia! Through faith, God gives us all the gifts that Jesus has won. Praise God! That beautiful message sings in us, in what we think and say and do. La, la la! We give God heartfelt worship, we are thankful God's gifts, and we are willing to show God's love to others. Amen!

Journal:

As God's child, you get to imitate His love. Write about how you want God to help you do that.

Pray:

Dearest God, when I hear how much You love me, I can't help but praise You. Thank You for putting Your song of salvation inside me. Bless my words that they may sing out what You have done. In Jesus' name I pray. Amen.   L. M.

WEDNESDAY

Acts 1:6–11

Cloud Watchers

Have you ever watched the clouds float slowly across the sky? Sometimes, you can see shapes in the clouds like rabbits, dogs, or houses. The clouds form and then reform into something else.

In our Bible reading, the disciples were watching the clouds. Jesus had led them out to Bethany. He had promised them that soon the Holy Spirit would empower them to speak the Word of God. He had commanded them to go into all the ends of the earth witnessing for Him. Then He had ascended into the sky. What did the disciples do? They stood watching Him until a cloud covered Him.

Maybe they were waiting for Jesus to come back. Maybe they were so amazed that they could not move. Anyway, they just kept staring until two men in white stood next to them. The disciples did not even seem to notice at first. Then the men in white spoke to them and wanted to know what they were looking at.

If you've ever been caught daydreaming, you know how they probably felt. They probably felt embarrassed that they had been caught staring at the sky. They were confused and wondered when Jesus would be back and afraid of what the future would bring.

The two men in white said Jesus would come back the same way He left. That was all the reassurance the disciples needed. After that, they returned to Jerusalem and waited to start their ministry to the world.

We, too, have that same reassurance. Jesus will come back. We do not have to be confused and wonder about it. He will be back. Until that time, we have the assurance that He is with us every day in our Baptism and in His Word. These things make it possible for us to be His witnesses to the ends of the earth and in our own neighborhoods.

Journal:
List all the places God has sent you to live or visit.

Pray:
Dear God, thank You for sending Jesus to die and to rise so that my sins could be forgiven. With my new life in Christ, give me Your power. Send me to love others as I am able. Amen.   C. H.

2 Corinthians 3:12–18

Superpower

Bright orange cape. Lightning blue suit. Silver gloves. Shiny black boots. Are you picturing a courageous superhero in your mind? If you could be a fictional superhero, what would your costume look like? What would be your superpower?

Comic books and cartoons are full of stories about heroic characters fighting bad guys. We are amazed at the unique powers that each has. Some can see through walls with x-ray vision; some can climb up buildings. Others can even transform from one shape into another. Many of them try to solve big problems, but none of them could ever solve the problem of sin. Only God could do that.

In some ways, God is like a superhero (though He's much more powerful!). Through Jesus, He defeated our greatest enemies: sin, death, and the devil. Not with a "Pow" or a "Bam," but by His holy, precious blood shed on the cross. Through Baptism and His Word, He has given you His victory and placed His "superpower"—faith—in you. And this superpower can transform you!

The Spirit of God helps us in all things. Instead of cheating on a test, we try our best. Instead of being greedy, we gladly give to others. Instead of denying our sin, we confess it. As we rely on God and are declared righteous by Him, He transforms us to become more like Jesus.

While God may not wear a bright orange cape, He is the *greatest* Superhero. And through His Spirit, He has given us His superpower.

Journal:

Write about some ways you could spend more time in God's Word.

Pray:

Most merciful God, forgive my sins for Jesus' sake, and through the power of Your Holy Spirit, continue Your transforming work in me. Amen.

L. M.

God's Heart, Your Heart

When you think about the word *heart*, what comes to mind? A muscle that circulates blood? A pink and red Valentine's Day card? The place where you put your hand when you say the Pledge of Allegiance?

Your heart is a very special part of you. It's more than just a place for fuzzy feelings in February. Your heart is where you feel happiness, guilt, love, and sometimes sadness. It is part of who you are, and it affects everything you do.

When you were born, your heart did not know how to love God. You were sinful and self-centered. You couldn't help it. You learned to look out for yourself, to cry when you needed something, to fuss over situations. You thought you were alone to figure out life. That's the sad truth but not the entire story.

Think about your favorite fairy tale. Does it include the main character "falling in love" with a wonderful prince or princess? That's what happened to us, to God's people. God heart was so in love with us that He sent Jesus to be our Savior. That's right. He sent His only Son to fulfill the Law.

Here's the next part of the story. When we became God's children, He put His love in us. He made us new people who could love Him and others. We got the power to love, even though we are still sinners.

However, while our hearts still beat, temptations will still come. The devil will lie to us and tempt us to love other things more than God. So we need to guard our hearts and minds. We need to be careful what we watch and who we hang around with. And when we do sin, we can ask God to forgive us. Remember the Lord loves a contrite heart. We ask for forgiveness "so that Christ may dwell in [our] hearts through faith" (v. 17).

Journal:
How do you plan to guard your heart and mind?

Pray:
Loving Lord, thank You for the gift of love. Amen.　　　L. M.

12 Romans 10:14–15

Beautiful Feet

I smoothed out my red dress and wound my hair into a tight bun. I looked down at my figure skates. They were polished and beautiful, with perfectly white laces.

Ever since I was a little girl, I had danced around on the slippery kitchen floor. I'd hopped onto the frozen puddles next door to try out my new skates. I had dreamed of performing in front of hundreds of people to inspiring and pretty music. Little did I know that my dream would come true.

Many people thought I'd be a missionary, a deaconess, or a worker in the Church. They weren't sure that being a figure skater would serve others in God's kingdom very well. Sometimes, I wondered if they were right. But then, God showed me something wonderful!

I learned that all types of people, with all types of jobs, can serve in God's kingdom. This meant that I put on Christ everywhere I went, especially at the rink. I was able to tell figure skaters and hockey players about the Savior! And I skated in front of many people to songs about God's love.

Our Bible reading speaks about those who proclaim God's Word. It says, "How beautiful are the feet of those who preach the good news!" (v. 15). Even though you aren't a pastor, you have beautiful feet. You are God's child with Good News to share. My feet have skates on them. What's on your feet? Skateboard shoes? Cowboy boots? Baseball cleats? Dress shoes? Flip-flops?

There are so many people who haven't heard about Jesus. God has chosen you to walk among them, to show them God's love. He has made your feet beautiful for His mission—no matter what you put on them!

Journal:

Read 2 Corinthians 5:20. Where has God made you His ambassador? Write about those places in your journal.

Pray:

Lord, help me to spread Your Word, right where You've placed my feet. In Jesus' name I pray. Amen.   L. M.

Colossians 2:9–10

Puzzle Pieces

Nadia smiled. She had worked all afternoon on the 100-piece puzzle. It was a picture of four chestnut horses running through a meadow. And it was almost done! All she had to do was . . . wait! There were no more pieces, but there were three empty spaces! She sat back disappointed. The picture just didn't look right with so many missing pieces.

When you became a child of God, He made you complete. Our Bible reading says that "you have been filled in Him" (v. 10). Before you knew God, you had empty spaces inside of you. Now, He has filled them. Through faith, He has put Christ in you, cleansed you, and is preparing heaven for you!

God made your salvation complete, full, without anything missing. But what about the puzzle of your life? The picture of your life still has many pieces to be put in place. You already have some of them, like the one for when you were born. And the ones for your first day of kindergarten and your seventh birthday. But it may look like there are a lot of pieces that aren't in place yet. There's high school, college, getting a job, getting married . . . so many pieces!

Don't be afraid that God will leave the puzzle of your life with missing spaces. He sent His only Son to die so that He could make you complete. He won't forget to make the picture of your life complete too. In fact, He has an amazing plan for your life! And He will be with you along the way as new pieces fill in more spots in your life.

Journal:

Write a prayer to God. Tell Him what scares you about the future. Ask Him to help you trust Him.

Pray:

Dear Jesus, thank You for filling me from empty to full with Your salvation. You make me complete. As I grow older, continue the good work Your Spirit has begun in me. In Your name I pray. Amen.   L. M.

Near the Shepherd's Heart

One year, I dreaded going to school. In fact, this was the year I was going to a new school. Everything about it seemed horrible. On the morning bus ride, I would scoot close to the window. Reaching for my backpack, I'd search until I found my Bible. There was one verse that would always help me—Isaiah 40:11. I would picture myself as Jesus' little lamb.

Have you seen paintings of shepherds? Usually, they are walking in front of their sheep or standing among them. But the Bible gives another picture of Jesus, your loving Shepherd. It's not enough for Him just to lead you where you should go. He wants to do more than that! He bends down, gently picks you up, and carries you close to His heart.

Can you think of a time you were frightened? Perhaps it was when you went to a new school, had changes at home, or moved to a different place. All of those things can be scary, especially when you feel alone. But Jesus doesn't ever forget about you! To Him, you aren't one sheep in a crowd of millions. You are the lamb next to His heart.

When I started my new school, it was in town. I had gone to a little country school all my life. The change made me feel small and unnoticed. Those were the messages I said to myself. But when I read my Bible on the morning bus, I didn't feel alone. I heard God's Word. He told me that Jesus, my Savior and Shepherd would rescue me from danger and carry me through that day and on into eternity.

Journal:

Describe a time when you felt scared or alone and God helped you.

Pray:

My Shepherd, thank You for making me part of Your flock by bringing me into the family of faith. Thank You for carrying me close to Your heart. Amen.   L. M.

Filtered

The mechanic finished working on Timmy's mom's car and came over to where they were waiting. Holding out what looked like a round accordion, he said, "Here's the part I took out."

"What is it?" asked Timmy as he studied the dirty black object.

"It's an air filter," the mechanic explained. "It keeps your engine clean by removing the dirt from the air. This is the reason your car has not been running smoothly."

"We have a water filter on our faucet in the kitchen, but it doesn't look like that," said Timmy.

"Well," the mechanic laughed, "if you took it apart, there would be something similar inside. Your house's air conditioner also has a filter. It doesn't quite look the same, but all filters do the same thing. They are designed to remove dirt from something like air or water."

In our Bible passage for today, David asks God to cleanse him with hyssop so that he will be clean and whiter than snow. Hyssop was a plant used in a cleansing ceremony. When lepers who were free of their disease came to the high priest, he would dip the hyssop in blood and sprinkle the blood over them. Hyssop carried the blood that showed the leper was free from his deadly sickness.

Jesus has cleansed us from our deadly sickness of sin. When He died on the cross, He became our sacrifice. His blood was sprinkled out when He died. He removed our dirty sins from us. He took our sins upon Himself. Through Him, we are clean.

Journal:

What are some things that need to be cleaned? Don't forget to put your name on the list.

Pray:

Dear Lord, thank You for sending Jesus to give Himself as my sacrifice and make me cleaner than even the purest snow. Amen.   C. H.

WEDNESDAY

THURSDAY

Our Own Trail of Tears

In the 1830s, the Cherokee (also called Cherokees) had a thriving, well-organized community. They lived where present-day Tennessee, Kentucky, North Carolina, South Carolina, and Virginia meet. They had been trading with the white settlers for many years and had a good relationship with the European settlers. They had a government in which leaders were elected by their own towns. A Cherokee man named Sequoyah invented an alphabet for his language. Many Cherokee were wealthy, owning homes, plantations, and farms.

However, soon everything changed. The white settlers wanted the Cherokee land. Some men in Washington DC decided the Cherokee had to give up their land and move west to Indian Territory in Oklahoma. The Cherokee did not want to leave. They had worked hard to make nice homes. Soon, though, soldiers came, and the Cherokee were forced to leave.

Thousands of Cherokee set out for Indian Territory in 1838. Winter came soon, and many died of disease. Food and water ran out. Many were too weak to make the long trip. When some of them finally reached their destination, they were not welcomed by others living there. They called this sad journey their "Trail of Tears."

Because of sin, death, and the devil, we are on our own trail of tears. Bad things happen daily. We have problems at school or at home. Friends hurt us. We experience lying, pain, and tears.

Our tears, however, will not last forever. God sees our pain and provides a way out. Jesus died for sin and rose again. God gives us faith in Jesus through His Word. Now we can look forward to a time in heaven when there will be no more tears. There, our trail of tears ends forever.

Journal:

How is Jesus with you on your trail of tears? How does He sustain you?

Pray:

Dear Father, thank You for walking with me on my trail of tears and for giving joy through the gift of heaven. In Jesus' name I pray. Amen. C. H.

Proverbs 18:10

Run and Hide

"Ha, ha, ha!" Colter rolled on his back, roaring with laughter.

"What's so funny, young man?" Mom asked as she walked into the room.

Colter could barely get the words out: "I . . . I hid behind the grandfather clock when Nate came out of his room. And I jumped out and scared him half to death! What a scaredy-cat! He's such a baby!"

Mom frowned. "Follow me," she said. Soon, Nate, Mom, and Colter sat together on the floor. "Do you think it makes Nate a scaredy-cat because he ran and hid?" Mom asked.

Colter looked down at the carpet, "Well, yeah . . . kinda."

"Boys, there are times when running and hiding does not make you a scaredy-cat or a baby." Both of the boys looked up at Mom with confused faces. "Even when you are grown up, there are things that might scare you. You won't know what to do. And you will just want to run and hide. When those times come, it is okay to run . . . as long as you run to God."

"How can we do that?" Nate asked.

"By praying and telling God you are scared. He will hide you in His arms, just like I'm doing right now." She hugged them both.

Tears formed on Colter's face. "But what if you did something wrong? Will God still want you to run to Him then?"

"Of course," Mom said. "That is especially when He wants you to come to Him. In fact, He is waiting to hear your confession and ready to forgive you for Jesus' sake!"

"I think I always want to run to God," Colter said.

"Me too!" shouted Nate.

Journal:

What are some ways you can "run" to God?

Pray:

Strong Lord, You are my safe place. In You, I find protection, strength, and forgiveness. I love You, Lord, and pray in Jesus' name. Amen. L. M.

Unique Voices

Jonathan saw a black head with two dark eyes rise above the water. "I see one!" he shouted, pointing across the canal.

"You're quite an expert at spotting alligators, Jonathan," said Uncle Ralph. "We'll have to bring you to the Everglades more often."

Alligators swim easily. They can jump as high as six feet and run on land between twenty-five and thirty miles per hour. They are fierce predators. The adults have no natural enemies except larger alligators. The babies, however, have many enemies.

The female alligator uses leaves, twigs, and mud to build a nest on the ground. She digs a hole in the center of the mound and lays a lot of eggs. Then she covers the hole with dirt and stays near the nest to guard it from any predators.

After about seventy days, the baby alligators begin to yelp and grunt from inside of their eggs. As soon as the mother alligator hears them, she recognizes their voices and starts scratching the dirt off the top of the nest. Many of the babies hatch out of the eggs by themselves, but some need help. The mother rolls these eggs around in her mouth until the egg cracks and the baby is freed.

Our Bible verse tells us that God knew us even before we were born. God is all-knowing. He is better than a mother alligator at recognizing His children.

Before Jeremiah was born, God had a plan for Him. You may wonder if God has a plan for you. He does—a special plan. In Baptism, He marked you as His. He freed you from sin, death, and the devil and gave you power to live under Him in His kingdom.

God planned for Jeremiah to be a prophet. What are His plans for you? I don't know, but God does. And He is leading you.

Journal:
What are some things God has for you to do today?

Pray:
Dear Lord, You know each person You have made. Thank You for making me in a special way and remaking me to be Your child in Baptism. Bless all I do today. In Jesus' name I pray. Amen.   C. H.

Acts 2:1-4

Unity and Peace

Every two years, the world celebrates the Olympics, alternating between the Winter and Summer Games. Several months before the opening ceremony of the Olympics, a torch is lit in Athens, Greece, where the Olympics began, using the sun's rays and a mirror.

From one to another, athletes pass the torch and carry it throughout continents. Finally, on the day of the opening ceremony, the torch enters the arena where the games will be held. Then the games begin.

The torch represents the unity and the peace of the Olympic Games. It is a visual way of showing that, at least for a few days, the competing countries unite for a common purpose.

Today is Pentecost. It is a special day in the life of the Christian Church. In fact, it is the beginning of the Christian Church. Today, we thank God that He sent the Holy Spirit to the Church.

On that first Pentecost, the disciples were gathered in Jerusalem. Suddenly, they heard a sound like a strong wind. The sound filled the whole house. Tongues as of fire came to rest on each of them. The Holy Spirit filled the disciples. They spoke about Jesus in other languages.

Although the Olympic torch represents unity and peace among the nations involved, that peace and unity does not last. Disputes break out and arguments arise, sometimes even during the Games. Family and friends, neighborhoods and cities don't have peace either.

By nature, we are enemies of God. On Pentecost, when the flames of God's Spirit arrived, the message of what Jesus had done on Calvary's cross brought true unity and peace. The Holy Spirit brings us God's peace. The Holy Spirit makes people holy and brings them to faith in Christ. We can trust, rejoice, and find comfort in Him—the one who brings unity and peace.

Journal:
What does Titus 3:5 say about the Holy Spirit?

Pray:
O Holy Spirit, thank You for making me holy by bringing me to faith in Christ, that I might be saved. In Jesus' name I pray. Amen.   C. H.

SUNDAY

20 Mark 1:29–31

Healed to Serve

"Mom, my head hurts," Audra called. "I have the chills."

Audra's mom came into the room with medication and a glass of water. She helped Audra sit up in bed and take the medicine. After Audra finished the glass of water, her mom sat on the side of her bed and gave her a hug. "I'm sorry you are not feeling well, Audra, but you'll get better soon."

Audra's mom was right. Later in the day, Audra felt better. She was so thankful her headache was gone that she felt like helping. She picked up towels from the mountain of laundry on the table and started folding them.

In the first chapter of the Book of Mark, Jesus began His ministry on earth. After teaching in the synagogue, He went to stay at Simon and Andrew's home. When they got there, Simon's mother-in-law was sick in bed with a fever.

Jesus went to her. He took her hand and healed her. Simon's mother-in-law got up. She was so thankful that she felt like helping. She immediately began to serve her guests.

Jesus knows when we are sick. Sometimes, He heals us immediately from our illnesses. Sometimes, He doesn't.

There is one disease we all have. Jesus took care of it. He stretched out His hands on Calvary and died on the cross for the sins of the whole world. In the healing waters of Baptism, He gave us His cure for our sin-sick lives.

Now, each day, we rise as forgiven sinners. We are free from sin's deadly consequence. We are free to serve. What could you do with this freedom? I don't know, but look around. You will find some way to thank God by serving others.

Journal:

Make a list of all the things you have to do today. Put a cross by each one. Just think, you can serve others through each of these tasks.

Pray:

Dear Jesus, thank You for healing my sin-sickness. In thanks, I want to serve in Your name. Amen.   C. H.

Matthew 6:25–27

Tender Loving Care

The emperor penguin lives in Antarctica. In May, just as winter becomes frigid, the female penguin lays one egg. After laying the egg, she carefully transfers it to the webbed feet of the male. Then the female travels to the sea, where she can feed on fish, squid, and shellfish. After building up her energy, she will return.

While the female is gone, the male cares for the egg. He uses an extra roll of skin and feathers to cover the egg on his feet. The male penguins huddle together and wait for the chicks to hatch.

After about sixty days, the chicks (also called fledglings) hatch. They remain on their father's feet in the brood pouch for several weeks. Once they can regulate their own body temperature, they move around on their own.

The young chicks do not worry about what will happen to them or whether they will have food. Their parents take good care of them and provide what they need. That's the way God planned to care for them.

How does God take care of you? God gives you everything you need. Absolutely everything. Do you deserve it? No, you don't. No one does. It may seem like you do since you may work for an allowance and try to be nice to others—at least most of the time. But you could never be sinless. You could never earn God's goodness. So, why is God good to you or to anyone?

God is good to you because He loves you. He loves you so much He gave you Jesus as your Savior from sin. God also gives us food, clothing, friends, teachers, pets, time to play, and a family.

You may worry about grades, friends, or your looks. In our Bible reading from Matthew, God says we don't need to worry about those things. He reminds us that He cares for even the birds. If He does that for birds, He will also care for His beloved children.

Journal:

Draw a penguin. Beside it, write something you learned today.

Pray:

Father in heaven, You have given me everything because of Jesus. Help me to see Your goodness. In my Savior's name I pray. Amen. C. H.

W
E
D
N
E
S
D
A
Y

Don't Deny It

Lucas was walking around the neighborhood, talking with his friends. Suddenly, Damean interrupted Lucas's thoughts. "Hey, Lucas, isn't that where you go to church?"

Lucas felt his face get hot and his heart started to pound. The people he was with were not "church friends." In fact, he had heard a couple of them laughing at what they called "church-going goody-goodies." But here was St. Paul Lutheran Church right in front of him.

"Yeah, I go there sometimes—when my parents make me," Lucas stammered. The truth was that Lucas went to church and Sunday School every week with his family. In a few weeks, he was going to help teach a VBS class of four-year-olds.

"I'm glad my parents don't make me go to church," Damean laughed. "I think it would about kill me to have to sit still that long."

"Yeah, it can be boring sometimes," Lucas agreed.

At first, Lucas felt like he handled the situation okay. After all, he didn't exactly lie—he just stretched the truth a bit—and things were still cool with his friends. They hadn't made fun of him at all.

Later on, though, Lucas felt guilty. He had denied his faith and, in doing so, denied Christ. That night, Lucas prayed and asked God to forgive him and to give him courage to stand up for his faith.

The Bible tells the story of another person who denied Christ. After Jesus was arrested, Peter denied even knowing Jesus three times in one night. When he realized what he had done, he cried bitter tears.

The good news is that Jesus doesn't deny us. He loves us and forgives us when we ask for forgiveness time after time. Because of His love, we can find courage to take a stand for Him. After all, He took the ultimate stand for us on the cross.

Journal:
Who are your friends? List them in your journal. Pray for them.

Pray:
Dear Jesus, please forgive me when I deny You. Give me courage when I speak about my faith to my friends. Amen.   M. W.

Light

It was January 1856. Abbie Burgess watched the storm. Her father had gone to a nearby island to get medicine, food, and oil for the lamps. Abbie was in charge of her sick mother, two younger sisters, and the lighthouse.

Abbie lived on a rocky, dangerous island known as Matinicus Rock, Maine. Abbie's father said he would be gone for one night, but because of the storm, he had already been gone for almost four weeks.

Abbie was exhausted. Each day, she filled all the lanterns with oil, cleaned the lenses of the lights, trimmed the wicks on lanterns. She scraped ice off the windows. Then, at night, she watched over the lanterns to make sure their flames did not go out. Without the lights, which Abbie kept burning, the ships were helpless. The dark waters hid jagged rocks or sandbars. There was no radar or sonar. Ships depended on lighthouses to protect them from possible dangers.

In our verse for today, Jesus speaks to the church leaders. He tells them He is the light of the world. He says that all who follow Him will not walk in the darkness. Some of the people in the crowd were in serious danger; they thought they could save themselves by doing good things. Others were in danger because they did not know Jesus was the Messiah God had promised.

Jesus is God. Through His death and resurrection, He protects us from the darkness of the devil, who hides the rocks of sin and the sandbars of death. Jesus' death and resurrection lights the way to heaven. Jesus' light is given to each of us in Baptism, through which we are given His power to "have the light of life."

Wherever you go today, remember that Jesus, the light of the world, goes before you. Pray that He will deliver you from all evil.

Journal:

Today there are many people who don't follow Jesus. Identify some of those religions in your journal.

Pray:

Dear Lord Jesus, You came into the world to redeem me. May the saving light of Your sacrifice shine in and through me. Amen.   C. H.

24 2 Chronicles 20:17–23

The Sentinel

Danger approached. The sentinel sounded the alarm. Each family member of his tunneled into the ground. It is what meerkats do.

Meerkats are members of the mongoose family. The one-foot- tall animals live in South African scrublands. They live in families or large groups of up to forty. They are community minded. Each group has several guards, or sentinels. These guards stand up firmly on their back hind legs and survey the area. These guards watch for predators. When they spot an enemy, they sound the alarm.

In 2 Chronicles, the Israelites are facing a large army. In fact, three large armies combined forces to make war on the Israelites. God's prophet told King Jehoshaphat that he and his people should stand firm and see the deliverance of God. When the day of the battle came, the Israelites saw God fight for them. Praising God, they marched out to their position but did nothing. When they got to the battlefield, the war was already over, and their enemies had been defeated.

Like meerkats and Israelites, we face many dangers. We face bullies and bad-mouthing. We face teasing and torment. We face failures and flops. When dangers come near us and we are helpless, we can confess our weakness. We can pray to God for help. We can read His Word. We can remember the promises of our Baptism.

Through the strength of God's Spirit, we can stand firm. Why? Because our warring enemies are powerless. Jesus defeated them all—sin, death, and the devil. He beat them all when He died on Calvary. Now, His victory comforts us. His victory makes us shout like Jehoshaphat's people, "Give thanks to the LORD" (v. 21).

Journal:

Write about a time when God delivered you from an earthly enemy.

Pray:

Dear Father, thank You for sending Jesus to fight for me. Deliver me from anyone or anything that would take away my faith in You. In Jesus' name I pray. Amen.   C. H.

2 Corinthians 3:18

Transformation

Spring is my favorite time of year. The world is transformed from death to life. Plants come to life. A small flower called a crocus begins the parade. Sometimes, they bravely bloom while there is still snow on the ground. Next, come daffodils and then tulips and flowering trees. Soon, the yards, gardens, and orchards look alive again, bursting with color. Birds make nests and lay eggs. Gardeners plant potatoes, onions, radishes, and peas. Children delight in outside fun—flying kites and swinging bats.

There was a time when we were as dead and dark as a gray winter day. When sin entered the world, so did death. Sin separated us from God, from His light and life. Our future looked dismal. But God promised a Savior who would restore life and take sin's punishment.

Christ's death and resurrection brought springtime back into our lives. When Christ died, He took our sin to the cross with Him. When He rose again on Easter, He guaranteed our salvation. Now, through His Spirit, we are transformed from sinners to saints.

In Baptism, our new life began. Through faith in Jesus, we received the forgiveness of sins and life forever. We received God's Spirit, who works God's good in us.

When you look at the flowers and trees around you, let them remind you of God's change in you. As the grass, flowers, and trees transform before your eyes, remember that God's Spirit continues to transform you!

Journal:

Draw some of your favorite flowers to remind you that God is working in you.

Pray:

Dear Jesus, thank You for transforming me in Baptism from death to a new life of faith. Amen.   M. W.

A Faithful Star

"Wow, Dad, look how bright that star is!" Jared pointed to a large star. He and his father sat outside swinging on a summer evening.

"That's Polaris, Jared, and it's also called the North Star. It was an important star for sailors for many years."

"Why would sailors care about that star?"

"The North Star is the brightest and closest star in the direction of the North Pole. Because of its location, it leads sailors to the north. Sailors sometimes called it the Steering Star."

"Wow, Dad. Does it still work today?" Jared wanted to know.

"Well, yes and no. Yes, the star is in the same place and can guide to the north. It is constant and faithful. But today, few people follow stars. Most sailors have radar and sonar to guide them. Something else is different today. Because of new and improved telescopes, astronomers found that what looked like one big star is actually three stars, close together."

"Ooh, that reminds me of God," Jared said. "He is three persons: Father, Son, and Holy Spirit."

"Right, Jared. The North Star reminds me of God in another way."

"Let me guess. The North Star guided the sailors. God, through His Word, guides us to salvation in Jesus. The North Star kept sailors going the right way. God's Spirit keeps our faith in God strong."

"And do you know one more way the North Star is like God?"

Jared thought while Dad went to get a Bible. "Here it is in Psalms. David says that God's steadfast love reaches to the heavens. His faithfulness reaches to the clouds."

God is faithful and constant just like the North Star. He is always there for us, always guiding and loving us.

Journal:

Draw a star. Beside it, write today's Bible verse.

Pray:

Heavenly Father, You are faithful and constant. Through Your Spirit, keep my faith in You strong. I pray in Jesus' name. Amen.   C. H.

Romans 8:28

Seeing Open Doors

Volleyball tryouts had just finished. There were twelve spots on the team; fifteen girls had tried out. Some girls would soon be sad. Coach was talking to each girl individually. Megan sat silently, praying. When coach called her name, Megan's skin felt prickly.

"Megan, I'm really sorry," Coach began. "I know you wanted to be a part of the team, but it won't happen this year." Then Coach paused. "I know it might not make you feel better now, but I've found that when the Lord closes one door, He opens another one. Maybe He has something else in mind for you."

Megan nodded, muttered a tearful thank-you, and left. The next day, she noticed signs at school announcing auditions for the musical. "You should try out," Megan's friend said.

"Well, maybe for the chorus, but only if you try out too," Megan responded.

Three weeks later, the girls were busy with rehearsals, getting costumes, and practicing lines with other cast members. It was about then that Megan saw Coach Wallace one day after school. "Coach, I'm glad I saw you," Megan said. "You know what you said about the Lord closing one door and opening another? Well, He did!"

"I'm so happy for you, Megan," she said, "I hope you can always remember that the Lord loves you."

"Thanks, Coach. I'll try." Megan smiled at Coach Wallace. "Well, got to go. I have a rehearsal now." The two parted, each with a smile.

Because we are God's children through Jesus, we can be sure that He can use even our disappointments to redirect our lives for good purposes. Even in sadness and weakness, God is at work.

Journal:
Write about a disappointment in your life that became God's blessing.

Pray:
Dear Lord, thank You for knowing what's best for me. Give me power to trust You and place my disappointments and hurts in Your hands. In Jesus' name I pray. Amen.   M. W.

28 Psalm 32:7

Our Hiding Place

Men pushed an iron ball into the cannon. Another man stood behind the cannon and lit the fuse. Boom! Swoosh! The cannonball shot across the field.

Lila and her family watched a reenactment of the Battle of New Orleans. That battle between the United States and the British Empire was part of the War of 1812.

The Battle of New Orleans took place on January 8, 1815. On the American side were about 2,500 untrained troops under General Andrew Jackson. On the British side were 8,000 well-trained troops. No one expected the Americans to win.

The British marched across open fields in bright red coats, playing music on their bagpipes. They marched in rows, standing tall and trying to scare their enemies. The Americans didn't fight like that at all. They hid behind dirt walls, shooting from their hideouts.

The battle was short. Many British soldiers died. Many Americans were saved by dirt walls.

Battles have gone on for years. In the Old Testament days, David was chased by the king and his men. David found a place to hide, and he found someone in whom He could hide—someone stronger than he was. In our psalm for today, David calls God his hiding place. David turned to God for protection.

You and I have enemies too. Some of them are mightier than we are. But God is stronger than all of them, and we can hide in His Word and promises. When sin or Satan attacks us, we can remember that Jesus has defeated them.

Journal:
Write today's Bible verse in your journal. Circle your favorite part.

Pray:
Dear Father, I could never face life's troubles by myself. Thank You for hiding me in Your arms and giving me Jesus' victory. In His name I pray. Amen.   C. H.

John 14:25–27

Attention, Please

How would you get someone's attention at a noisy shopping mall? Perhaps you might wave your hands wildly in the air. Or maybe you would give a yell or a whistle. What about if you were in a quiet movie theater? Would a yell or a whistle be appropriate there?

Do you think God ever has a problem getting our attention? We are so busy that we forget His Word. We are busy with art projects or book reports. Busy with baseball or gymnastics. Busy with piano recitals or clarinet solos. Busy reaching a new level at exciting computer games. But right now, God has your attention. You are listening.

Before His death on the cross, Jesus told His disciples that He would get their attention through the Holy Spirit after He was gone. God would send the Holy Spirit to remind them, to coach them, to strengthen them so they could proclaim what Jesus had said and done while on earth. After Jesus ascended into heaven, the disciples were filled with the Holy Spirit at Pentecost.

The Holy Spirit works in you too. He gets your attention through God's Word and in Baptism. If you have received instruction in the Lord's Supper and are able to participate in it, God works in that Sacrament too.

Because of our sinful nature, we are tempted to ignore the Spirit's call to be God's children, to hear His voice, and to live His way. When that happens, God's Spirit doesn't give up on us. He wants our attention. He gives us eyes of faith so we can see our sin. He leads us to confess that sin. God forgives us and continues to love and renew us each day.

Journal:

In your journal, write about the work of the Holy Spirit. What does He do? How does He work?

Pray:

God, help me focus on all that You have for me to do today. Through Your Word, give me just what I need now and always. In Jesus' name I pray. Amen.

J. D.

Give Thanks to God

Maggie squealed with delight when Grandma handed her the wrapped package. Grandma and Grandpa had bought a gift for their granddaughter while on vacation. After Maggie opened the gift, her mother coaxed her, saying, "Maggie, what do you say?"

Maggie wasn't sure. So she said, "What is it?" Maggie's mother wasn't expecting that reply. She wanted to hear "Thank you" come out of Maggie's mouth!

Sometimes, we forget to say thanks when we receive a gift. We especially forget to thank God. It's easy to take for granted all the things He gives us. God blesses us continually, often without hearing a "thank You" from us.

Today's Bible verse might be familiar to you. Perhaps you've used these words as a table prayer before or after a meal. That's great, but giving thanks to God can go beyond mealtime. God gives us more than just food and drink. Think about it. He blesses us with jeans, tennis shoes, and jackets. He provides a bed to sleep in and good books to read. God gives us special places too, places like churches, schools, parks, and movie theaters. He gives us parents, pastors, teachers, friends, neighbors, and cousins. The list of His gifts could go on and on.

Along with these blessings, God gives us greater gifts—such as the forgiveness of sins. God's promise of forgiveness lasts forever because He sent His Son, Jesus, to die on the cross in payment for our sins. When we have forgotten to thank God or we find ourselves sinfully thinking that we deserve good things, we can tell Him we're sorry. Once again, God gives us just what we need—His forgiveness.

Journal:

Write today's Bible verse in your journal. Won't it be fun to thank God for the many blessings in your life?

Pray:

Dear good and glorious God, thank You for richly blessing my life. Make me more aware of these blessings, that I might thank You for each one. In Jesus' name I pray. Amen.   J. D.

Wait for the Lord

Only one word could describe Mrs. Caruthers's morning: terrible! Her alarm clock did not go off. She lost a contact lens. A button fell off the skirt she was planning to wear. The toaster burned her breakfast, and she barely missed the mailbox as she pulled out of the driveway. Mrs. Caruthers knew her day couldn't get any worse! Or could it?

The train crawled by the crossing at an unbelievably slow rate. Of all days to be stopped at a train crossing! Almost in tears, Mrs. Caruthers thought of how much had happened to her in the last hour. Now, to top it all off, she sat motionless, waiting for the slowest train in the world to pass by.

The wait at a train crossing can sometimes be unbearable, especially when we're in a hurry. There's no way to make the train go faster. We just have to sit, be patient, and wait for the train to go by.

Sometimes, waiting for the Lord to act in our own lives feels the same way. We want the Lord's answer to our need immediately, but that doesn't always happen. Months, weeks, or even a few days can seem like an eternity to wait for an answer to prayer. The Lord wants us to wait for His perfect timing. Jesus completed God's perfectly timed plan when He died to save us from our sins. Through faith in Jesus, God's promise of forgiveness is ours. Even in our most selfish moments, God waits to offer His merciful love and forgiveness.

The next time you are stopped at a train crossing or waiting for your dad to pick you up after practice, think about the Lord. Thank Him for the unexpected opportunity to talk to Him in prayer. Ask the Lord for patience while you wait for Him to do the right thing at the right time.

Journal:
Write down when and where it is hard for you to wait.

Pray:
Dear Lord, give me patience as I wait for You. Show me how to appreciate each moment You've given me and to wait for Your perfect timing. In Jesus' name I pray. Amen.   J. D.

FRIDAY

May Journal

1

2

3

4

Happy Spring!

5

6

7

8

9

Happy Spring!

20

21

22

23

24

Happy Spring!

25

26

27

28

29

Happy Spring!

30

31

Drawings